WINNING THE BACKDOOR WAR

JONATHAN GAINSBRUGH

Bulk price discounts are as follows:

No. of Copies	Price
1 copy	$14.95 + 10% s&h
2-5	$11.95 + 10% s&h
6-10	$ 9.95 + 10% s&h
11-20	$ 8.95 + 10% s&h
20 plus copies	$ 8.49 + 10% s&h
100 plus copies	Call or write for quote

ACKNOWLEDGMENTS

There are so many people to thank that I feel inadequate for the task.
I would like to thank all those who have had a part in this ministry,
stretching back over the past several decades. Your help has been
noticed by me, but most importantly by our loving Heavenly Father.

To all our wise-hearted Board and elders, to all of our Partner Pastors
and their churches and missions heart missions boards.

To all our pastor friends and ministry partners across the country, who
have invested shoulder-to-shoulder with us for years, and once again
have given to make this equipping and ministry and book possible.

Most of all I would like to thank the world's most wonderful wife,
my wife Jeanette, and the world's four best kids: our daughters Heaven,
Christmas, Grace, and our son Christian.

Most of all I must recognize and thank the Lord Jesus Christ, for
Whom I minister, Who gave His life for me, and without Whom I would
have no life, ministry or eternal hope and joy.

For all those whom I have not named, I especially point to Jesus' own
words in the scripture that contains His rewarding promise:
"he who gives even a cup of cold water in My Name to one of these
little ones who believe in Me...they shall in no wise lose their reward."
Mark 9:41

Preface

I look forward to you, the reader, gaining the maximal amount of information and transformation from your time spent reading the following pages.

Much of this material is not new with me. A great debt of gratitude is due to the forerunners of this volume on Assimilation. My thanks go out right at the start of this book, to those who have written classic, seminal works on this vital, vastly unknown and under-appreciated subject.

In order, I would have to include: among these seminal works:

"Assimilating New Members"	*by Lyle Schaller*
"Attracting New Members"	*by Robert Baste*
"Apathetic & Bored Church Member"	*by John Savage*
"Beyond Church Growth"	*by Bob Logan*
"Church Growth Ratio Book"	*by Win & Chip Arn*
"Dying for Change"	*by Leith Anderson*
"The First Year",	*by Suzanne Braden*
"Helping your Greeters Give a Warm Welcome"	*by Dale Cobb*
"New Member Assimilation"	*by Joel Heck*
"Prepare Your Church for the Future"	*by Carl George*
"Welcome	*by Ervin Stutzman*

I have committed myself (under God's leading) to read ALL of the classic works in print in the field on the subject of Assimilation. As I have read these many dozens of books, I noticed recurring themes and materials freely borrowed and reworded.

Duplicated "core" materials would repeatedly show up. This lead me to realize and know once again the universal truth of the statement: "Material from one source is what some call plagiarism,......but quoting five or more sources is called something different.. something called "RESEARCH".

I have tried to not only list my source books, but to give credit through-out to them.

In the thirteenth century in Europe, a plague known as the "Black Death" swept the entire continent. The Bubonic Plague literally wiped out tens of millions of European inhabitants. The name "Bubonic Plague"(its medical name 'Yersinia Pestis') comes from the buboes or skin lesions that came from fleas biting humans. However, it was only carried by fleas from infested rats. Biting the rats infected the fleas, and down-line the fleas killed millions of humans.

The flea was the "connective" element in the disease chain. Blaming the flea alone, or the rat for that matter, would not sufficiently link the cause with the fatal end results. This disease was prevalent in the non-hygienic society back then. Currently it is totally preventable, although the CDC(Center for Disease Control) in Atlanta reports occasional rare cases in New Mexico, Colorado and Arizona.

Germs have not always been a commonly known and respected reality. In fact, Louis Pasteur (around the year 1860-1865) was mocked by those that first heard his theory that germs and micro-organisms in non-pasteurized milk commonly carried deadly and crippling diseases into the human body.

He introduced the concept of little "microbes" invisible to the natural eye. That which is now commonly believed was openly ignored and mocked back then in those initial days of medical learning.

The dynamic vs. linear-grid in Church-work

There are always people at either end of any linear/dynamic spectrum. While some try to work "rote" formulas, others just as disastrously attempt to do all church work "by the Spirit" without letting the Holy Spirit anoint their minds, strategies, brains, and plans, to produce "anointed thinking".

As you read this book, pray over its contents with an open mind to what God's Spirit would say, regarding change and improvement of the way church-work is done at your church.

An incredible lack of Assimilation teaching is a major problem in the American church today. "Front-door Fixation," and its fraternal twin " Back-Door Blindness," are leading causes of shocking casualty/fatality statistics in American Christianity.

Statistics reveal 85 of 100 American churches are in a plateau or decline mode. Tragic, but true.

To help churchmen and pastors "Win the Back Door War" and "fix the leaks in their buckets" is the intent of this humble work.

Once again, my full gratitude and thanks to my mentors, instructors, and many sources.

Table of Contents

Table of Contents
Continued

SECTION V - Back Door #4: New Members

SECTION VI - Back Door #5: Regualr Members

SECTION VII - Back Door #6 & #7: Inactives & Dropouts

SECTION VIII - Tracking and Implementations

Chapter 1

Welcome To The Back Door War!

There is a war going on, round the clock.

It is a silent war, taking many prisoners, destroying much good work, and leaving in its wake many casualties and fatalities. It is an unseen, almost subliminal war that needs to be brought out into the open if it is ever to be won.

This war affects every church in America, and every church in the world. Therefore, this vital war also affects every believer in America, and in the world as well.

Although every church suffers from this warfare, most churches and pastors have not been equipped to win the battle.

This book, based on an entire semester Bible school curriculum, is founded on the concept that we can all "work smarter."

The Back Door War can only be won through a thorough understanding of Assimilation. This vital subject of Assimilation, in the church world, is something like Rodney Dangerfield. His famous line is, "I can't get no respect."

Assimilation seems to be way down the "totem pole" of ecclesiastical importance. Yet, it is indispensable in winning this silent war that like a plague of locusts devours so much of what every church works so hard to gain - its new growth.

The back door war can be won. Arming yourself and your church through reading and implementing this book puts any reader well on his or her way.

"Semester In A Day"

This book, and the seminar on which it is based, is a synthesis of a twelve week Bible College full semester class taught at Capital Bible Institute in Sacramento. You have heard the education phrase "intensives", which enable a person to gain a full semester of credit in a condensed eight-hour a day Monday through Friday one week, or three, or four weekend "intensive" format. This book, and the seminar, are both an "intensive's intensive".

The comprehensive materials you learn in this book cover information ninety percent of all ministers were never taught.

The seminaries and Bible colleges never taught it to them. This is not the ministers' fault; however, the buck must stop somewhere. Too commonly, a course in Evangelism is included in Bible school and seminary core curriculum. Rare, however, is the Bible school that includes a full semester course on Assimilation, teaching ministers to preserve the "front door" fruit they spend their entire lives producing.

Ministers and Bible schools suffer from a lack of information many are not even aware exists. INFORMATION DOES EQUAL POWER. Jesus Himself said, "You shall know the truth, and the truth shall set you free," (John 8:32). Assumptions won't set us free; sincere belief in inaccurate or untrue information won't free people; belief in generations-old myths can't set us free either.

Only the truth will do that.

None of the above items are what Jesus said would free us. Jesus said, "Only the Truth will set us free." Hosea 4:6 says, "My people perish for lack of knowledge." Knowledge is not our enemy: lack of it can be, though. This verse in another translation reads, "My people are silent for lack of knowledge."

Lacking knowledge can keep God's people from both speaking about, teaching and addressing Assimilation problems and solutions.

Chapter 2

"Idea Bank"

This page is designed to be used as an "idea-bank" to help you list and return to the most impactful ideas you run across while reading this book.

Benefit even more from this idea by reproducing the "idea bank" form onto a standard 8 1/2" x 11" sheet or merely enlarging the "idea-bank" grid on a copier. Keep the sheet separate, tucked into the book as a detachable "Idea Bank."

One might use a post-it memo, or 3x5 cards and a highlighter, to help refer back to specific pages to reconsider ideas you have written down.

The four vertical columns at the top of your "Top Idea-Bank" page give some time-phasing as you write down ideas, resources, etc. Because every church is unique, define Immediate, Short, Medium and Long-range "time-windows" as appropriate.

Some may time "Immediate" as a week, while others will time it in the next month. One reader's "idea bank" may concentrate on New Convert ideas, while another's may concentrate on Pre-Visitor and Visitor ideas.

Romans 12:1,2 commands "be transformed by the renewing of your mind."

Reader: what massive benefits could every church receive if each reader of this book took a prayerful posture at the start of this book, giving God a signed "blank check" for whatever change and improvement He might put in to, or take out of, your Christian life, church work, and ministry?

Idea Bank Page

Use this page to keep track of the top ideas God gives you while reading this book.

IMMEDIATE	SHORT TERM	MEDIUM RANGE	LONG TERM
1.	:	:	:
2.	:	:	:
3.	:	:	:
4.	:	:	:
5.	:	:	:
6.	:	:	:
7.	:	:	:
8.	:	:	:
9.	:	:	:
10.	:	:	:
11.	:	:	:
12.	:	:	:
13.	:	:	:
14.	:	:	:
15.	:	:	:
16.	:	:	:

Abraham, Sarah and Isaac: A "Long-Term" Idea and Promise

While Short and Medium term seem simple enough, one last input on the time columns. "Long term" might be ideas to implement beyond one year.

God spoke long-term to Abraham. In Genesis chapters 12 and 15, God promised a child to Sarah and Abraham. He just didn't tell Abraham exactly when. Abraham and Sarah were 75 years old at the time of the promise. After a thirteen year wait, they carnally attempted to receive the promise through Hagar, resulting in the birth of Ishmael ("the wild man").

But God's long-range promise still wasn't yet to be. Isaac, the child of the promise, wasn't to be given for 12 more years. That means the promise to Abraham was given 25 years before it was realized. Now I call that a "Long-Term" project.

A Few Sample Idea Bank Projects Might Include:

Immediate: Writing and requesting regular mailings and catalogues from specific cutting-edge Information Age ministries listed further along in this book.

Short Term: This might be to both order and read a certain book that I recommend on catching the "new realities", such as Leith Anderson's "Dying For Change", or "A Church for the 21st Century".

Medium Range: Ideas might include attending John Maxwell's Leadership seminar, or going to Willow Creek's Church Leadership Seminar.

Long-Term: These ideas could include hosting an equipping Assimilation seminar such as my "Winning the Back Door War" seminar at your church, etc.

Chapter 3

General Secretary's Report

In the August, 1991, issue of the Pentecostal Evangel, the U.S. Assemblies of God fellowship's major weekly magazine, was a revealing article.

This report was a statistical extract given out at the 1991 Biennial General Council to which the 11,600 American Assemblies of God churches send their pastors and delegates.

In this report, the Executive General Secretary gave some vital information. Looking closely at these statistics gives some handles to lift out statistical extract as to what the numbers really say.

Statistics commonly make people's minds "go blank" or into "overload mode".

I am going to pull out a few statistics to illustrate the drastic need for "Winning the Back Door War".

Conversions

One of the reports subheadings lists conversions.

 # l: Total Conversions Reported

In plain English were are told that in 1989 and 1990, 571,000 conversions were reported. This is over half a million converts a cause for much celebration regarding Kingdom growth over the preceding two year span.

It then states that during calendar year 1991, churches reported 320,000 conversions, an increase of 70,000 over the preceding year.

2: Sunday Morning Attendance Increase

The next subheading is, "Increase in Sunday A.M. Worship Attendance". Here, we're plainly told that Sunday morning attendance in 1990 increased by only 28,000.

Total conversions of 320,000 in 1991 only produced a Sunday Morning Worship attendance increase of 28,000

Subtract 28,000 (Sunday A.M. increase) from 320,000 (the 1991 new convert total); differential: 292,000. The question must be asked, where are the other 292,000 converts reported in 1991?

The "retention-dimension" lens on this reveals that it took 100 converts for the movement as a whole to post a Sunday morning increase of nine. Put another way, for every ten converts, Sunday morning increased by one person or less. If one buys 100 loaves of bread at the supermarket, but arriving home only finds ten left to put in the breadbox, is there a back door, or tailgate problem?

If a third of a million babies are born into a family or nation, shouldn't that number affect the total population?

If ten babies are born in a family, shouldn't the family population a year later be increased by more than one? Where are the other nine?

No hospital or family would tolerate the "infant mortality rate" these figures portray.

Now before getting hyper-critical of this one fellowship, obtain and extract figures, both for your fellowship at large, and for your church specifically.

Determine the number of converts posted, and the Sunday morning growth figures. Subtract the one from the other, and you can tell how wide the New Convert Back Door is in your own backyard.

The Back Door War needs to be won in every church.

Credentialing of New Ministers

Next, lets look at the 2,089 new ministers credentialed.

With a ten-year goal of credentialing 20,000 new ministers, we are told that we hit the 1991 portion of that goal, or over 2000 ministers - precisely, 2089.

Now, of course, we lost a few ministers during that same one year period. This is reasonable: some died, some moved away, and others may even have left the ministry, with perhaps a few joining other movements.

Nonetheless, if we gained 2089 new ministers in 1991, what was the number of ministers lost?

The number lost was... 2,036!

Subtracting losses of 2,036 from a gain of 2,089, net gain was only 53 ministers - a mere 1.7 percent increase or retention of loss to gain. When compared to the 28,000 ministers in the movement, it is less than a .001 of one percent increase.

In 1990, the average was less than one new minister for each of the 56 separate districts in the United States.

Every business person knows if he doesn't get a bottom-line figure of gains and losses, it will close you down.

New Churches Planted

One more area of back door loss.

Why bother about "Winning the Back Door War?" Here's why. During 1990, 359 Assemblies of God churches were opened. Some churches also had to be closed during that same year of 1991. How many closed?

The Secretary's report tells us we closed 179 during 1991.

Round these figures from 179 to 180 (total churches closed) and round 360 churches planted up to roughly 365 (or one a day). We can easily see a ratio of planting one new church every day and closing one roughly every two days.

Another way of putting it would be: "Today, plant a church, tomorrow plant a church, but also bury one." Basically, two steps forward, and one step back.

No one would attempt a 20-mile hike walking forward two miles, then backwards a mile. To accomplish the 20-mile distance this way would actually involve walking over 30 miles or 50% more.

Losing a church every other day, year round, is too high a price. There's a Back Door War to be won here as well.

Leaky Bucket Graphic

Notice the graphic of the two buckets.

If two ranchers are pumping ten gallons of water into two buckets, but one bucket is losing five gallons a minute from a leak in it, one rancher would unquestionably be "WORKING HARDER, BUT NOT WORKING AS SMART" as the other rancher.

Which bucket would a smart church be: Bucket A, without the leak, or Bucket B, with the leak?

Bucket A's pastor is a smart pastor, working just as hard as Pastor B, but producing much more for God's Kingdom.

Chapter 4

Basic Assimilation Scriptures

Readers at this point may be saying to themselves, "Where's the Bible in all of this? I'm a Bible believer! Find the word assimilation in the Bible, or any mention of one back door, much less seven!"

Proverbs 27: 23-27

Perhaps the single most powerful scripture on Assimilation is Proverbs 27:23, which reads, **"Be thou diligent to know the state of thy flocks, and look well to thy herds."**

Continue reading the next four verses to the end of the chapter (vv. 24-27):

"Riches do not endure forever, and a crown does not secure for all generations. When the hay is removed and new growth appears, and the grass from the hills is gathered in, the lambs will provide you with clothing, and the goats shall be for the price of a field."

It is obvious that the "lambs" mentioned here are connected with financial provision. This passage mentions them being "for" the acquisition of buildings, materials, and for clothing for the household.

"You will have plenty of goat's milk to feed you and your family... (provision and nutrition) to nourish your servant girls."

Obviously, financial provision is not any believer's main concern, nor mine. However, let me ask, how many readers would mind if their church (or ministry/missions) budget this next year increased by 50%.

Right here in these verses, God tells those with ears to hear that if one diligently pays attention to the state of his flocks and herds, God will bless many dimensions of their life and ministry, including finances and provision.

Luke 15: The Diligent Shepherd and the 99

A major scriptural theme relating directly to Assimilation is God as our Great Shepherd, and Jesus as the Good Shepherd (John 10, I Peter 2:25). In the Twenty-third Psalm, we all know the passage, "The Lord is my Shepherd..." Many other scriptures talk of a shepherd who takes good care of His sheep (Psalm 100, all of John 10, etc.).

In Luke Chapter 15, Jesus tells three parables, namely, the Lost Coin, the Lost Sheep, and the Prodigal (or lost) Son.

In Luke 15:7, Jesus tells us "a certain shepherd had 100 sheep. At the close of one day he realized he had only 99 of his 100 sheep there in the safety of the fold."

Jesus preceded this story telling about a woman with ten valuable coins. Somehow, she misplaced one. The woman, Jesus says, lights a lamp, sweeps and searches the entire house until she finds it. One valuable coin missing (1 out of 10) was a mere 10% loss factor. The point of the story is that Jesus commends the woman as diligent because she both NOTICES THE LOSS, and SEARCHES for the coin UNTIL SHE FINDS IT.

She isn't satisfied until she has ten out of ten. A mere 10 % loss factor, meaning a 90% success rate, is not set forth as success here by Jesus, although it is an "A" in most classes. Jesus commends the woman because she finds the other 10%.

The Diligent Shepherd

A second example in Luke 15 is the story of a diligent shepherd. Jesus tells us this shepherd has 99 sheep. How did this shepherd know there were only 99 sheep that evening, and not the full flock of 100?

Did he say to himself, "Ah, the flock just feels like 99,"? Did he run a UPS bar code scanner hooked up to a satellite uplink to obtain and read his nightly hi-tech print-out?

No!

Did he just assume that because there had been 100 sheep the day before, there obviously had to be 100 sheep 24 hours later?

Once again, no!

We know the shepherd had to use the "C" word - he had to count them. He was missing one sheep, only one missing out of 100. He had a seemingly successful 99% retention rate which left him with a very slight 1% loss factor.

Jesus commends the shepherd as DILIGENT!

He does not commend the man because the man says, "I am doing fine, I've only lost one sheep. Dear Lord, bless 'Sam the Lamb'; help him, Lord, give 'Sam the Lamb' supernatural strength to fight through the wolves," or, "send a supernatural star to guide him back to the flock, and Lord, I'll give you all the praise. Amen!"

No!

The diligent shepherd in Luke 15 does something practical, spiritual, and effective. The shepherd leaves the 99, goes and searches for the lost sheep until he finds it.

Does he abandon the 99? Does he leave them totally unprotected to be ravaged by predators, while he searches for the one lost lamb? Obviously not! He doesn't sacrifice the 99 for the 1, but neither does he cling to the 99 and let the single lost lamb perish. He diligently cares for both. Jesus powerfully and clearly commends his diligence.

In Luke 15: 7-10, Jesus tells us, "There is more joy in Heaven over one lost person that repents and finds salvation, than over 99 righteous who have no need of repentance."

"Be thou D-I-L-I-G-E-N-T!"

"Be thou diligent to K-N-O-W the state of thy flocks..."

To "K-N-O-W" is not to assume, guess, or presume!

Having the information this diligent shepherd bothered to get on his flock is vital. Up-to-date, precise information can provide POWER to enable us all to be commended by our Lord.

Only a 1% Loss Factor:

Only a 1% loss factor, and yet the diligent shepherd is able to not only notice it, but to correct it.

Would you like your church ministry to receive commendation like the shepherd Jesus commends in Luke 15? Wouldn't any church like to have assimilation procedures to pick up a 1% loss factor among new converts, and new or regular members?

Aha! I thought so. Congratulations! That's what "Winning the Back Door War" is all about.

Ezekiel 34

This single Old Testament chapter more closely parallels Jesus' denunciation of the Pharisees in Matthew 23 than any other. In Matthew 23, Jesus says repeatedly, "Woe unto you, Scribes and Pharisees..." Ezekiel 34 is that chapter in the Old Testament. Here, God clearly says, **"Woe to the shepherds of Israel, because you have not brought back that which drifted away, you have not bound up that which is wounded, you haven't fed the starving, or brought back that which was driven away."**

"Not well done, No-good and unfaithful servant!"

Ezekiel 34 is not about God saying, "Well done, good and faithful servant," as Matthew 25:21 states, and as we all hope one day to hear from our Lord's mouth.

Ezekiel 34 is really the opposite. Instead of being "DILIGENT" these shepherds are NON-DILIGENT, lazy, slothful, etc.

Sometimes we can define a thing not only by what it is, but by what it is not. The shepherds in Ezekiel 34 were NON-diligent.

God says, "I will take care of My flock, and I will draw them

to Me. I will create for Me shepherds who will love My flock."
(Exekiel 34:11,12) God wants to teach us to improve our caring
for His flock.

Shouldn't every church be able to detect a 1% loss factor? If
you were the missing sheep, the one out of a hundred... or if the
missing lamb was our wife, child, brother, sister or loved one,
wouldn't we want a church to be able to track and recover that one
percent loss?

Jesus died for that one percent. With His divine help, we can
stop that loss. No church represented by anyone who ever reads
this book can say, "We have only a 1% loss factor or less." How
many would like to get it down to one?

If they were worth dying for, they are worth counting,
tracking, nurturing, and keeping.

Matthew 9:12-13

In Matthew 9:12-13, Jesus defines His mission as being sent
"not to those who are well, but to those who are sick."

Who are the people usually exiting a church's back doors?
The well or the sick? Is it the emotionally and relationally whole,
or those that are hurting, broken, sick, and bruised?

"Holy Spirit, speak to our minds, teach, prompt and convict
us to want to do better. In Jesus' Name and for His sake. Amen."

Chapter 5

Defining and Redefining Assimilation

Our next subject is another key to winning the Back Door War. We must define the subject of Assimilation - what it is, and what it is not. What exactly is this vital dynamic so under-prioritized in the Body of Christ?

Your Definition of Assimilation

Write down in the blank space provided below exactly what you believe Assimilation is. Keep it under a dozen words.

Assimilation is: _____

_____

I believe every person in every church ought to be able to fill in that blank above. A few shorter definitions I've been given by some pastors are:

Assimilation is:

A) "Two or more things acting or looking alike"
B) "Getting the people involved"
C) "Integrating people with God and the local church body"

Webster's Definition

Let look at Webster's definition. It reads:

I.   Assimilation is... "The act of bringing or coming to a resemblance." It comes from the Latin words 'a' meaning "to or toward," and 'similar' (a verb: to become similar to or like). Assimilation is bringing people closer to a resemblance of.

Through centuries of usage, the word clapboard became the word cupboard. The dissimilar 'p' sound next to the 'b' was eliminated and assimilated to become like its neighbor, the 'b'.

II. A secondary dictionary definition for Assimilation is the "digestive usage", which reads, "to change digested food into part of the living organism."

We're all familiar with having food in our stomachs that just didn't seem to want to assimilate. We then feel queasy. We feel like we're going to lose it, one way or another.

III. The third and final Webster definition is to "take something that is separate, and make it a part of the whole."

Shorter Definitions of Assimilation

Sometimes the shorter a definition we give something, the easier it is to latch onto. Below are a couple of short, classic definitions:

1) "Taking people from wherever they are, and making them an active, healthy, on-going part of the local church."

Taking people from wherever they are means they might be Pre-Visitors, they might be New Converts, New or Regular Members; it might even be Inactives, or Dropouts.

One more super definition is, **"Making insiders out of outsiders."** This is another way of saying, "Making participants out of spectators."

One, Two and Three Word Definitions

Several good one-word definitions might include: "Incorporation", "Interweaving", "Absorbing", "Inclusion", "Disciple-Making", and "Blending". Notice that most of these are verbs ending in "-ing", denoting an on-going process, not an event with a beginning and an end.

Some two-word definitions might include: "Becoming family", "Relational Nurturing", and "Intentionally Including".

We must let people know they're part of the family. Folks need to know they are welcomed and needed.

Finally, a few good three-word definitions might be: "Becoming one with", "Including, not Excluding" and "Bringing into oneness".

Chapter 6

Twelve Basic Understandings About Assimilation

So far, we've only discussed very foundational things. Putting in the foundation of a house, digging out the footers, constructing the concrete forms, mixing and pouring the concrete are definitely not the most exciting parts of building a house. Not much to proudly show for one's effort. No shouts of joy until it's done.

Yet, it is that same, boring, unexciting foundation that determines the height of the building to be built. Following are twelve basic understandings, foundational to truly realizing what it will take to win the Back Door War at your church.

Understanding #1:
Assimilation is an On-going Process

Assimilation, even more than evangelism, is a process, not an event. It is not a "done deal" at some point in time. No matter where a Regular Member may be in position to your church, he not only may, but W-I-L-L disengage, without on-going care.

Understanding # 2:
Assimilation-Understanding is Progressive

Assimilation is progressive in understanding. No one person knows all there is to know about the subject. However, as we learn and study, we progressively understand more and more about it.

Understanding # 3:
"Assimilation is Multi-Dimensional"

Assimilation is intriguingly multi-dimensional, much like music. Music is both a science and an art. There is a deeper, linear, "music theory" dimension of music that the great composers Beethoven, Tchaikovsky, Bach, Handel and others studied to augment their natural giftings and abilities.

Like music, assimilation has its own language. We are going to learn some of this language, words you may not have heard before; words like "stick rate", "psychographics", "paradigm", "disengagement", "psychological contract", and scores more.

Understanding # 4:
Assimilation Illiteracy is Widespread

There are 30 million functionally illiterate Americans. We may know some of them, but they do not want their illiteracy known by us, although, of course, it is no fault of their own.

When my son was younger, he hadn't yet learned how to swim. He dreaded getting into the swimming pool when other kids his own age were around. When only adults were around, he didn't mind doing the doggy-paddle. But among his peers, he wouldn't go in the pool.

Assimilation illiteracy has a similar unacknowledged effect. It is rampant, but hidden, and somehow has been "driven underground." The "retention dimension" is unknown territory to most pastors.

When asked, "How much of your church's harvest are you retaining?" or, "What percentage of your first-time visitors do you retain?" or, "What percentage of New Members do you lose annually?", most pastors have no solid, quantitative answers.

While most pastors have taken Bible school classes in evangelism, fewer than 10% have ever taken a class in assimilation. Asking this question at seminars I teach, fewer than 5% raise their hands signifying a "Yes."

A class on assimilation should be required at all Bible schools and seminaries BEFORE anyone is launched into full-time ministry. I wrote this book hoping it will be used someday along with Lyle Schaller's "Assimilating New Members" as curriculum in hundreds of Bible schools nationally and beyond.

Understanding #5:
Fog Addiction is Commonplace

By "fog addiction", I mean anything that clouds or obscures our vision in clearly seeing the Back Door problem and its causative parts. Like carbon monoxide, "fog" is unseen, non-odiforous (unsmellable), and 100% lethal.

"Replacement Growth" is a common example of "fog". Most people think their church is growing because they have 10 or 20 join as New Members every so often. All the while, they know the church is continuously losing people as well.

Win and Chip Arn in their brilliant book, "The Church Growth Ratio Book" (listed in Ordering Appendix in back), state that the average church loses a minimum of 10% a year. Common losses include:

1-2% loss factors through death;

2-4% transfer to other local-area churches;

2-4% move away to other towns; and

2-4% backslide or fall away from the faith.

Now if you realize a church of 400 loses 10% a year, that means they would lose 40 people annually. Gaining 40 people per year (admitting 10 members quarterly) only produces a plateau.

This is the illusion of "replacement growth". To actually grow by 10 %, the church would actually have to grow by 20% (since it is losing 10% day in and day out throughout the year).

Many churches are not growing, but think they are. Statistics tell us 85% of all U.S. churches are plateaued or in decline. Many of these plateaued churches are losing, not winning, their own Back Door War.

Understanding #6:
Assimilation is Quantitative

Quantification is merely a big word meaning one can numerically track or count it. A classic assimilation proverb is, "The less you track, the wider the back door will be."

Understanding #7:
Assimilation is "Relationship-Powered"

As Carl George, Bob Logan and others repeat so frequently, "People come to church for a variety of reasons, but they stay for primarily just one: relationships." The "R" word, "Relationships" is the reason. To spell evangelism and growth for any church in the 90's, spell it with an "R" for relationships. One can also spell "Evangelism" in the 90's with an "A" for "Assimilation." More than ever before, people are going to have to be assimilated through intentionalized relationships.

The "Growth through Evangelism" formula used to be, "Win them, then assimilate them." Now, the formula and dynamics are reversed. Most programs in growing churches today are designed to first "Assimilate people, then win them." That way, when you win them, they have the "relational atmosphere" to sustain and preserve them.

What a relationally sick world we live in: trial marriages, pre-nuptial marriage dissolution clauses, and a broken-heart harvest of 50% of all baby boomers divorcing each year. The average boomer is divorced by 34.

Yet, the doctor is not sent for the well, but for the sick. We have the medicine for those relationships. This generation was not brought up realizing, "All you really have are relationships."

Salvation, the ultimate relationship, is not a set of earth-bound, man-made rules, nor is it the "do's and don'ts" of religion. Those who have no relationship with Jesus are not those going to Heaven.

Understanding #8:
Assimilation Must Be Intentionalized

Assimilation works best on a pre-arranged basis. Systems must be designed and set up. It should start the minute someone drives into the parking lot, steps foot in the church, or before.

Understanding # 9:
Assimilation is Different From Evangelism

Assimilation is different, yet as much a part of the Great Commission as evangelism. Like body systems, both are vital. Respiratory, central nervous system, digestive, circulatory system, immune system - which one would you rather do without?

Each is equally indispensable and vital. So it is with both Assimilation and Evangelism in fulfilling the Great Commission.

Understanding #10:
Assimilation is Vital to Any Church's Growth Rate

Whether a church is truly growing and to what extent, assimilation has something to do with it. A church plateaus when its small groups are at saturation point. The fact that most Sunday School classes are not growing, just as most churches are also not growing, is directly connected to assimilational health.

Understanding #11:
Assimilation is "Information-Powered" and Question-Based

When we ask better questions, we will get better answers. Doctors train eight to ten years to become competent specialists. They are taught to ask certain questions, to track vital signs, and get adequate and precise information to prescribe the proper medicine.

Understanding #12:
Assimilation Tracking Must Be Intentionalized

The common cliche states that "the road to hell is paved with good intentions." God demands more than good intentions. Good intentions to provide diligent care for the flock of God must be made operational and become benefit-producing realities. An effective tracking system is indispensable to any and every church.

Chapter 7

Sixteen Myths of Assimilation

We have all, at least once in our lives, believed something...
only to find out it wasn't true. Sometimes this happens when a
meeting time and place is set. We assume the other person clearly
understood the meeting place and time. Later, we are disappointed
to find that what we assumed was so clearly communicated was
not at all what was understood.

A myth is a similarly untrue mental concept. In the fifteenth
century, most scientists believed the earth was flat, not round.
There still exists a society called the "Flat Earth Society". Today,
we know the so called "flat edge" of the ocean at the horizon is
really due to the curvature of the earth, and normally the ocean
horizon is approximately 12-13 miles away.

"Myth-busters" in days past were sometimes not only openly
ridiculed, but persecuted and even put to death for questioning
commonly believed "myths" that were really untrue. Following
are sixteen myths that help churches lose the Back Door War.

The Sixteen Myths of Assimilation

Myth #1:
Assimilation is God's sovereign work, not ours.

This is a common myth. Some Christians say, "The Holy
Spirit will do it. God will take care of it. He doesn't need our
help." But I Corinthians 3:9 states, "We are co-workers and co-
laborers together with God."

Yes, God is sovereign and does things we never could do. Of course, Jesus' words, "without Me, you can do nothing" are true. He does, however, frequently ask us to do our part as His helpers. In John chapter 11, at Lazarus' tomb, Jesus said to the people, "You roll away the stone, and take off the grave clothes." In John 6, Jesus told His disciples, "You give them food to eat."

Myth #2:
Assimilation is spiritual; therefore, it must be allergic to systems.

This myth cripples many people and many churches in their efforts to implement assimilation. This thinly disguised over-spiritualizing prevents the setting in place of the very tracking systems scripture and common sense requires to win the Back Door War.

Myth #3:
Assimilation is based on our assumptions which, of course, never need to be questioned.

The things we assume to be true are things we've usually never questioned. "We assume our converts are being taken care of," "I just assumed our visitors feel welcome and will come back," or, "I just assume new members will become a part of the church family," are common untrue assumptions.

I Thessalonians 5:21 states, "Prove all things." We must continually re-examine our assumptions, because they can unintentionally put us to sleep. Assumptions commonly allow us to be robbed blind through unexamined, preventable Back Door losses.

Myth #4:
Assimilation is the clergy's job.

Too many of God's people (both congregations and even more tragically, ministers themselves) believe ministry is strictly the clergy's job. They unscripturally see this as reason and justification for their salaries. The "Isn't that why we pay them?" myth leaves in its wake far too many "two man baseball teams" and "three man football teams."

It keeps millions of God's people sitting on the bench as "Pew Potatoes" or "Spec-taters", instead of participants in the ministry to which God calls each of His children.

Myth #5:
Our forefathers never needed it, nor did we. Why do they?

Many pre-boomers feel, "Why does this new generation need assimilation and 'relational pampering'? What's wrong with these baby boomers?"

Obviously, the "me generation" boomers do need help. Eighty million of them, with only 10% estimated to be in church, are creating 1.5 million additional divorces each year.

Since Jesus said, "The doctor is sent not to the well, but to the sick," (Matthew 9:12, 13), can we legitimately criticize a sick generation, rather than minister healing to them as the "extended hands" of the Great Physician?

Myth #6:
One size fits all.

Here's another popular myth. Jesus treated the people to whom He ministered uniquely and individually. With one rich, young "yuppie" (perhaps with his $50,000 hyper-luxury Lexus car parked outside) in Matthew 19, Jesus advised, "Sell your Lexus, give all to the poor, and follow me."

However, in John chapter 3, Jesus dealt with multi-million-aire Nicodemus, whom the Jewish historian Josephus tells us "could have fed all of Jerusalem's quarter-million people for three months with his personal fortune." Jesus never even mentions money or wealth in dealing with Nicodemus.

Obviously, Jesus treated wealthy people (and all people) individually. Clearly, to Jesus, "One size does not fit all."

Another part of this myth is the belief that "Targeting 'felt needs' isn't spiritual." Tell me William Booth was a compromiser, working by choice in the slums of London.

It was Booth who chose the twin slogan words for the Salvation Army, "Blood... and... Fire". It was also Booth who said, "When you preach a sermon to a hungry man, make sure you wrap that sermon in a sandwich."

Myth #7:
We're a friendly congregation.

Every church likes to fancy itself as the "friendliest church in town". Some churches actually believe it so much they take it to its totally illogical extreme which is, "We're so friendly, we don't even need to ask our visitors."

If they really believed that, they would ask the ultimate judges of that presumed friendliness - the visitors themselves.

Myth #8:
Churches don't pro-actively assimilate people. People assimilate themselves.

This is a deadly myth. Too many churches think people will assimilate themselves. Examine the number of visitors your church has and how many of them come back as second-time visitors (V-2's).

People do not assimilate themselves, as surely as food does not assimilate itself. Is it the food's responsibility to assimilate itself, or is it the responsibility of the body and the digestive system God designed within it? Of course, it is the body's responsibility. So it is with churches.

Myth #9:
If people don't feel at home here, God has another place for them.

Most often this myth works counter-productively to the desired outcome. If church shoppers "shop until they drop", where will they "drop"?

Obviously, they will drop where they feel the most comfortable. Making people feel comfortable, accepted, and loved, or "at home," is best accomplished by design, not by chance.

Myth #10:
We believe the numbers when they're good.

Many church people unconsciously subscribe to this myth. When a church is creating positive, growing numbers, it's easy to believe them. Some feel it is spiritual to believe the statistics when they're good.

However, when the numbers are not good, it is not only spiritual, but often a matter of life or death, to also believe them and act appropriately. To rationalize and say, "When the numbers are bad, statistics can say whatever you want them to say," is not sound thinking.

When a man's wife calls at work and says, "Little Johnny has a 99.7 degree temperature, please pray for him," Dad is polite and may say a quick prayer, then resume work. However, if Mom calls back an hour later, and says, "Honey, Johnny's fever has now hit 104.5 degrees"... the numbers are VERY negative, but they must be heeded.

It would not only be unspiritual to NOT pay attention to the numbers, it would be criminally negligent, tantamount to child abuse, and might even result in death.

Myth #11:
New Converts will somehow nurture themselves if their conversion is truly "real".

Tragically, too many churches believe this. Churches think to themselves, "Somehow, the new convert is going to make it to New Convert class."

Question: What single problem plagues practically every New Convert class in America?

Answer: Getting the New Convert to the New Convert class.

Whose responsibility is it to diagnose this, and create ministries that will effectively care for the New Convert?

Myth #12:
Joining our church as New Members and "belonging" are synonymous.

Lethal mythology once again! The "M" word (myth) quietly but effectively keeps this church Back Door wide open. Quite a good number of people join the average church. However, half of New Members never get to the place of truly belonging, and end up not even attending.

Myth #13:
People assimilate themselves naturally.

Basically, we're dealing with intentionalizing relationship development. Too many churches imagine, pretend, or incorrectly think it will happen automatically. It increasingly doesn't happen by accident.

Myth #14:
Assimilation is finished when someone becomes a Regular Member.

When someone survives the first twelve months as a New Member, they then become a Regular Member. Often, however, the unspoken dynamic is, "Okay, you're done." Assimilation is not done when someone becomes a Regular Member.

Myth #15:
When Regular Members go Inactive, they are betraying us.

Numerous church people subscribe to this myth, by saying to themselves, "Our Inactives need to repent! They betrayed us, and now they need to make all the moves back to us."

Myth #16:
Once people have dropped out, there's nothing more we can or should do.

This primary "dropout myth" not only keeps Back Door number seven open, it also prevents many valuable lessons from being learned.

All sixteen of these myths are commonly believed. They debilitate and retard the growth of far too many churches. The more of these myths any given church believes (and allows to be operative, whether actively or passively), the more these beliefs damage that same church, making it more of a victim, and less of a victor, in the Back Door War.

Chapter 8

Smart Weapons and the Gulf War Analogy

In January of 1989, when we entered the Persian Gulf War, our leadership sent 40,000 body bags, as well as 20,000 medical personnel.

It was Sadam Hussein who said, "Don't mess with me. I'm going to use nerve gas, chemical warfare, and more. The blood of your dead and wounded is going to measure up to the horse's bridle."

Thank God we had leaders like Norman Schwarzkopf and General Colin Powell who used strategic thinking, and non-conventional "smart weapons".

Traditional military wisdom would have sent in a massive ground assault. This is what Sadam wanted and was counting on. Our strategic high command didn't present a conventional ground assault. If they had, we would have filled thousands of body bags.

Instead, our leaders used what is now a household word: "smart weapons". We used an aerial assault tactic called "carpet bombing". We used laser-guided AGM-65 Maverick "smart-missiles" that have a target-seeking video camera built right into the missile's nose.

We, as a generation, saw video footage of a missile zeroing in through cross-sights on its ammunition factory target.

That "smart-missile", traveling at over 1,000 feet per second, was able to "thread" a 20-foot wide factory smokestack, because it was a "smart", not a dumb missile.

One key component of this smart-missile's technology is the video camera built into the missile tip. This video camera broadcasts visual flight-path image and target information to the computer screen in front of the pilot in the F-18 cockpit. Computers in the fighter plane continually receive information to correct, fine-tune and adjust the missile's path.

As Christ's disciples, we know Jesus our Lord wants us not to just "drop the bomb", but to hit the target. "Hamartia", the Greek word for sin, means to miss the mark, or miss the target.

There is a target in each community for every church to aim at and hit. Through the superior guidance system of the Holy Spirit, churches must examine their programs and weaponry in winning the Back Door War.

Every church can have "stealth" instead of "scud" thinking. Sadam fired scuds, but never really knew where they would hit. Some churches have scud thinking; others are using smart-weapons. Scud thinkers say, "Well, pastor, we never did it that way before. We never had to assign sponsors to New Members or New Converts," etc.

Many churches are using obsolete weaponry, and as a result are losing their Back Door War.

Chapter 9

The Vocabulary of Assimilation

There is a special vocabulary of Assimilation and Harvest-preservation. If I threw a quiz right now and said, "Explain the 'Background Theory', the 'Berry-bucket theory', 'Code of Silence', 'Disengagement Path', 'passive exclusion', or 'the six to eight week window'," most readers would not relish the resultant test scores.

Here are 150 phrases we'll cover in this book taken from the seminar on which this book is based:

Active listening
Affiliating stage
Affinity-based
Age wave
Agoraphobiacs
Alban Institute
Anonymity
Antipluralist
Anxiety-Anger Complex
Arn, Win and Chip
ASM Assimilation Theory
"At Risk" Period
Baby Boomers
Baby Busters
Back Door (verb)
Back Door Revival
Background Theory
Barna's Scorecard
Baste, Robert
Berry-Bucket Theory (5)
Biological Church Growth

Bonding
Braden, Suzanne
Burnout (prevention)
C.A.L. Principal
C.F.I.
Church Growth Ratio Book
Code of Silence
Cohesiveness
Commonality
Conflict Resolution Technique
Congruence
Connectedness
Conversion Growth
the "Convinced"
Cultural Overhang
Cultural Relevance
"Cutback Syndrome"
"D.O."
Decisioning
Demographic Information
Dethmer, Jim

Disengagement
Disengagement Path
Drop-outs
Drop-out Recovery Team
"Dropsy"
E-0, 1, 2, 3, Evangelism and Growth
Encrusting
Encrustment
Entry Path
Entry Points
Ethology
Exclusionary Factors
  (Active/Passive)
Exit Interviews
Expectations
Failure to Thrive
Feeding & Following
Fellowship Circle
Felt-need Targeting
Fog
Fog-Addicted
Fog-Busting
"F.R.A.N." gelism
Friendship Team
Friend (need for 7)
Front-Door Evangelism
Gatekeepers
George, Carl
Gift-based, Passion-driven
Glue (20 types)
"Glue-Testing"
"Grieving Period"
"Grieving Period" (transfer)
Heck, Joel
History Telling
Homogeneous Unit
Hospitality Mentality
Hospitality 7-Step Program
Hybels, Bill
Inactives (IA's)
"Inactive-itis"

Inclusiveness
Incorporating
Indigenous
Institutional Maintenance
Intentionality
Introversion
Jethro II
Jethro Principal
Koinonitis
Leadership Community
LLI (4 phases)
Law of 3.4 Hearings
Logan, Bob
Magnetism
Maslowe's Hierarchy
Maxwell, John
Meta-Theory
Mobilization
MQ—
Mortality Rate
New Converts (NC's)
New Members (NM's)
"Newberry"
New Member Abuse
Nucleate
"Older-Berry's"
P-1, P-2, P-3, Evangelism
Paradigm Shift
Parallelism
Pedagogical
People-Flow
Plateau and Decline Disease
  (P&D)
Pluralistic Pre-War Generation
Program Sanctuary Syndrome
Precipitants
Pro-Active
Psychographic Information
Psychological Contract
Quantify
Qualitative

Chapter 10

Identifying the Seven Back Doors

When presenting the seminar, I take the transparency of this church drawn with seven backdoors and put it out of focus. Many churches have their focus mechanisms too far out of visual alignment to win their Back Door War.

Speaking by phone once about my seminar with a Pastor/overseer of 15 churches, he said, "The difficulty with your seminar is that we don't have just seven back doors. We have so many back doors that we can't even count them."

My response was, "Well, if you host the seminar, perhaps we can at least get your Back Door count down to single digits."

The Five Blind Men and the Elephant

We all know the story of the five blind men and the elephant. Each was brought to try to identify and describe the huge creature. One blind man touched the elephant's side and thought it was a wall. Another grabbed a leg and thought it was a tree trunk. One felt the elephant's trunk and claimed it was a fire-hose, while one more blind man touching the elephant's tail felt sure he held a rope. Finally, the fifth blind man grabbed the elephant's tusk and thought it must be a wild bull.

How many of the blind men were right? Actually, none was.

Every church, is simultaneously losing people out of more than one back door. In fact, every church is losing people out of each of the seven back doors that follow here.

Closing Your Church's Seven Back Doors

TITLE	Backdoor 1	Backdoor 2	Backdoor 3	Backdoor 4	Backdoor 5	Backdoor 6	Backdoor 7
A							
B							
C							

The Seven Fold Grid

Let's look more closely at the seven back doors, and identify them.

Back Door #1: The Pre-Visitor (P-V)

Back Door #2: The Visitor (V-1, V-2, V-3)

Back Door #3: New Converts (NC)

Back Door #4: The New Member (NM)

Back Door #5: The Regular Member (RM)

Back Door #6: The Inactive (IA)

Back Door #7: The Drop-Out (DO)

In the next five minutes you will be able to repeat these seven back door titles forwards and backwards, along with their abbreviation codes.

On the accompanying "Seven Grid", let's fill in the blanks. First, for the purpose of accelerating the learning curve, I would like you to write them in. In the first box on line A, write in "Back Door name."

Back Door #1: Pre- Visitors

Before anybody visits your church, without exception, they will first be a Pre-Visitor. Some churches lose many people before they get in the door. I've seen people drive into an overcrowded church parking lot, cruise it, and then keep right on driving out the same entrance they just drove in through.

Back Door #2: Visitors

We will cover this area extensively, including topics like "What is the source of visitor flow?", "Who are most of your visitors?", "Why do they visit?", "Why do or don't they come back?," and "Why do certain visitors become V-l's, and then second, and third time visitors, etc.?"

Back Door #3: New Converts

Hopefully a number of unsaved visitors will visit enough times to become New Converts, giving their hearts to the Lord.

Back Door #4: New Members

New Converts, properly nurtured, will eventually want to become New Members.

Back Door #5: Regular Members

Regular Members need to be taken care of as well as Newcomers and Visitors.

Back Door #6: Inactives

The Inactive gives you a maximum of six to eight weeks to communicate with them regarding their specific reason for going Inactive, or they'll go out Back Door #7 and become Dropouts.

Back Door #7: Dropouts

The Dropout is to the Inactive what pneumonia is to the common cold. The best cure, of course, is prevention.

Every church must deal with all seven of these categories.

People used to die of now almost extinct diseases like measles. Aren't you glad your grandkids won't have to die from dyphtheria or small pox? People died of the flu (influenza is what they used to call it). Are you glad someone invented a vaccine to slow it down?

How about polio and tuberculosis? Polio crippled 27,000 children a year as recently as 1950. By 1974 the number of US cases had dropped to 7.

This book will help you learn how to identify and eliminate some common diseases in your church, diseases like visitor blindness, koinonitis, "Inactive-itis", "dropsy", etc.

Please repeat out loud and learn the names of these seven back doors now from one to seven. Now try to say the seven names backwards.

Next, please code the second line of the "Seven-Grid"

Living in the Information Age, we increasingly use codes. Let's relate this now to the Seven-Grid and these seven specific Back Doors. Learning to operate in "Code-mode" can save time in every area of your life. It will help you write notes to improve the retention of each of your church's Seven Back Doors.

The code for Back Door #1, Pre-Visitors, is "P-V"
The code for Back Door #2, Visitors, is "V-l, V-2, V-3."
(We will discuss in-depth, separate strategies for your first, second, and third time visitors.)
The code for Back Door #3, New Converts, is "N.C.'s"
The code for Back Door #4, New Members, is "N.M.'s"
The code for Back Door #5, Regular Members, is "R.M.'s"
The code for Back Door #6, Inactive's, is "I.A.'s"
The code for Back Door #7, Dropouts, is "D.O.'s"

We all know you can't operate a computer without codes. You have to use the eight-dot-three DOS code to name and list a file so the computer will work with it. It's part of the system.

In the Information Age, we as Kingdom people need more, not less, information. This one element, more than anything else in the world we live in, has changed.

Our Heavenly Father never changes. Our Lord Jesus is immutable, as Hebrews 13:8 tells us, "Jesus Christ is the same yesterday, today and forever." God's Word, the Holy Bible, never changes. Psalm 119:89 states, "God's Word is forever settled in Heaven."

Yet, while God never changes, culture does. When the Dutch landed in 1626, they bought Manhattan with trinkets and cloth valued at 60 guilders (or 1 1/2 pounds of silver... current market value $1,500). Obviously, no one buys any part of Manhattan with beads today.

To accomplish the same goal today, some new purchasing methods, strategies and materials would be indispensable.

If we tried to go into a store and buy stuff with the beads they used 300 years ago (even if you could find them), we would be culturally "out of synch" and out of luck.

Seven Grid 'Love-Relationship' Analogy

Horizontally, from left to right along the third line in the "seven-grid", we can continue this Back Door analysis with a "relationship-love-marriage (and tragically divorce)" analogy.

In every love relationship, there is a sequencing, a life- cycle progression and development. It is just as true in human relationship development between attenders and any given church. Before one progresses to the state of committing to be husband or wife, there are several predictable preparatory stages.

#1: Pre-Visitors: "Getting their attention"

For a Pre-Visitor to start a relationship with a church, one thing is required - the church must get their attention. No one has ever gone on a date with someone, who failed to first get their attention.

Many churches assume everyone in town knows who and where they are, and all of the good things their church offers. In most cases, this is more myth than fact.

2: Visitors:
"Attraction"

To get close enough to ask and obtain agreement to go on a first, then second and third date after getting a person's attention, there must be attraction: some type of magnetism or interest, to draw the person into even beginning the relationship.

3: New Convert:
"Deepening Affection and Commitment"

After several dates, an ongoing and increasingly deepening relationship develops. In the case of the New Convert, the commitment to each other perhaps could be compared to "going steady". Conversion must realistically be likened more to engagement at best, if not betrothal, but truly, short of the wedding and marriage.

A lot of people give their life to Christ, but never really get "married" to Christ. Too often, the "marriage" is over before the honeymoon is done. Folks too often go to the altar but somehow, they don't get the eternal, internal alterations.

#4: New Members:
Engagement and the "Honeymoon"

Following #1: attention, #2: attraction, and #3: continued affection, comes relational stage # 4: commitment and marriage. "Joining the Church Day", to the New Member, is truly similar to "marrying" the local church.

5: Regular Members:
Marriage, Maturity and Responsibility

The analogy continues. The "newly-weds" go beyond the "honeymoon-elation" stage and settle down to maturity, productivity, and to responsibly raise, support, and care for their family.

#6: Inactives:
Estrangement and Separation

Sometimes marriages break down. Usually, its a relational and communication degradation, occurring a little bit at a time. The number one cause of difficulty in marriages is not the lack of money, a new home, or a better car. **We all know that the number one complaint is a lack of communication.**

Most of us assume there is enough communication going on at our churches, but do those either now Inactive (or currently going Inactive) at only church feel communication really is sufficient?

7: Dropouts: Divorce

If the lines of communication aren't re-established, the ongoing conflict is usually not resolved. Instead it escalates and the opposite of resolution takes place. The situation and relationship deteriorates, and the Inactive becomes a Drop-Out.

Chapter 11

Pre-Visitor Introductions

Who are the pre-visitors outside any given church, or for that matter, across America in our current national culture. What are they thinking and looking for? What would draw them to a church? Why do they come, and why, more importantly don't they ever "darken the doors of a church"?

Many Churches are out of synch

Many churches are out of step, or "out-of-synch" with the new current realities their Pre-Visitors represent. An example? Statistics tell us 60% of the average church's visitors today are single. Since this is true, then why do only one out of six churches have any type of singles ministry at their church?

This is merely one example from many we need to discuss.

Name and Describe the Three P's of Evangelism

Peter Wagner teaches that evangelism must be examined more closely, to be properly defined in its three essential, phased elements.

P-l Evangelism is Presence:

The Presence of the Gospel in evangelism is illustrated perfectly by Jesus' words in Matthew 5:16 where our Lord said, "Let your light so shine before men, that they can see your good works, and glorify your Father which is in Heaven."

Thus, for a church to reach the secular, non-churched world, its good deeds must prove its divine mission and gain a hearing for the spoken part of its message.

P-2 Evangelism is Proclamation:

Proclamation, or preaching of the Word, is another type of evangelism embodied in so many scriptures. Mark 16:15, "Preach the Gospel to every creature," is perhaps one of the most well known P-2 verses. This, of course, is part of the gospel, but , contrary to some evangelism styles, O-N-L-Y a part of the whole definition of evangelism.

P-3 Evangelism is Persuasion:

Jesus commanded His disciples, not merely to perform good works, not merely to preach the word, but in Matthew 28:19-20, "go and 'Matheteusate panta ta ethne'... to make disciples out of all the nations (and people groups)."

Persuasion evangelism (creation and nurturing of ongoing, discipled fruit) is the ONLY legitimate aim of the other two P's of evangelism. Its aim in four words - "Lordship for a lifetime."

Do you have all three types of evangelism working interconnectedly, and in a proper balance, at your church?

Ask yourself which of the three types of evangelism, "P-1, P-2, or P-3" is most likely to impress and attract your local area's basic unsaved Pre-Visitor?

Which type of evangelism (P-1, P-2, or P3) do most churches rely too much upon, never truly reaching down, and reaching the mindset of their area's Pre-Visitors?

If there isn't sufficient P-3 nurturing and disciple-making, or enough P-1 "good works" Pre-Evangelism among the unsaved, what happens to a church's over-reliance on good-old P-2? If there is only P-1 and P-2, where is the "fruit that remains?"

Name Western Civilization's Three Main Paradigms

Can you name Western civilization's three major paradigm shifts? The word 'paradigm' means a major world view, a set of lenses, or understandings, a grid or map operated off of.

In Western Civilization (Europe and North America), the three major societal paradigms have been the Agricultural Age, the Industrial Revolution, and the Information Age.

In the Bible, the two major paradigms were the Old Testament, and then the New Testament.

Paradigm Blindness

Undeniably, the Scribes and Pharisees revered the Old Paradigm so absolutely that they developed "paradigm blindness." They blinded themselves to even the possibility of a new paradigm. They blinded themselves to the new Covenant of Grace, and its ultimate representative, our Lord, Jesus Christ. When Christ appeared to initiate the New Paradigm of God's love and mercy, salvation through His grace and shed blood, they refused to change paradigm.

Each of us, as our Lord's representative, must commit ourselves to learn to "read" and "play" (or maximally operate) the new Information Age paradigm we live in.

An Amish Analogy to Stimulate New Paradigm Thought

Recently, we took a family vacation and passed through Lancaster, Pennsylvania, the land of the Amish. My wife loves Amish people; they are dear-hearted and they love the Lord. However, are the Amish going into A-L-L the world and preaching the Gospel, making disciples of every nation?

They are easily one to two hundred years behind the times.

Now shift for a moment to the church in Europe. It is not just a hundred years behind. It is undeniably centuries, hundreds of years, out of touch. It didn't get that way in a decade or two. They had to work at it.

Let me ask, is Jesus out of date? Has He ever been, or will He ever be? No! Of course not! Jesus Christ never has been, is not now, and never will be obsolete, irrelevant, or out of date.

Why is it then that the majority of the unsaved and unchurched claim most churches are exactly that - irrelevant and out-of-date?

#3 How did the paradigm shift affect Charles Spurgeon's Church ?

In his masterful, best-seller book "Dying for Change," Leith Anderson shows how the paradigm shift from the Agricultural to Industrial Age very powerfully affected Spurgeon's great church. In 1854, Spurgeon was called to the great Metropolitan Tabernacle in London. He who now is known as the "prince of preachers", was then a 19-year old kid. Spurgeon preached the gospel, and eventually even the Queen of England came to listen, along with people from around the world.

God kept blessing, and eventually Spurgeon became the Paul Yonggi Cho of his day. His was the biggest church on the planet. They built Spurgeon a tabernacle that seated 5,000, and filled it twice each Sunday. The church grew to 15,000 members.

However, today if you go to "Charlie's Place," as it became known to cabbies all over London, now 130 years later, the same church and building exist. However, on any given Sunday morning, you will find only 76 people, meeting as a historical society.

Throughout the mid-to-late 1800's, the Western world was switching from a rural, agricultural paradigm to an urban, Industrial power base. People were moving from the country to the city.

Britain, which had ruled the world for two centuries, lost its paradigm, and its power base as well.

Many things have changed since then.

Metropolitan Tabernacle did not change with them.

The glory days of Metropolitan Tabernacle passed it by.

Europe, the "home of the reformation," is now the Earth's only completely "post-Christian continent," with only 2% of its population actively Christian.

Are the glory days passed for the Church of Jesus in America, and beyond? Ephesians 5:27 states that our Lord is still coming back for a "glorious church."

Leadership in Spurgeon's church refused to change with the times. Its glory-candle was removed, with only a shell, a memory, and building full of memories to remain.

4 What do the statistics tell us about Christianity in America?

Church statistics point toward the sad reality that Christianity is on the decline in America, even while it is on the growth curve elsewhere in the world. George Barna states that over $8 billion spent by U.S. churches in the last decade has not produced any appreciable increase in market share or attendance.

When President Clinton was elected in 1992, the cover of Time magazine read, "MANDATE FOR CHANGE!" People, unabashedly, voted for change.

#5 What benefit does all the talk and writing about megatrends hold for the church today?

Christian writings on Megatrends are absolutely vital. Despite this fact, many church folk are "stuck in the mud," refusing change, and embodying their favorite song, "We Shall Not Be Moved." The world around them is changing more rapidly than ever before.

Louis Pasteur was ridiculed when he went public introducing the theory of microbes, germs, and unpasteurized milk. Critics scoffed, "Ah ha! Tiny things crawling around under this so-called 'microscope' of yours, germs that give diseases to people. Hah!"

We should be grateful Pasteur wasn't stopped by the mockers. Jonas Salk studied the mold on bread, and eventually discovered both penicillin and the Polio vaccine. Some people must have mocked him, saying, "You're crazy! What a foolish waste of valuable time, studying moldy bread in a laboratory setting. That won't help anyone."

Because he didn't stop, children worldwide don't have to fear the crippling disease of polio.

Not everyone senses the need for "megatrend sensitivity," nor will they in your church. Nonetheless, smart Christians intentionally need to become pro-active toward current and future change, rather than being "re-active" and living in a never-ending "catch-up" mode.

Analogous to tuberculosis and polio, there are diseases that cripple churches. God is calling leaders among His people to discover, invent and innovate new "vaccines and cures" to protect and preserve both churches and their fruit.

#6 Can you define Baby Boomers? Why are they the largest unreached people-group in America today?

There are those who don't like all the talk about "Baby Boomers". Some old-timers feel, "Let them do it our way, or let them go elsewhere." That is not even close to the heart of Jesus.

There are 80 million Baby Boomers born between the years of 1946 and 1964. The phrase "Baby Boomer" came from the "Baby Boom" that occurred in America immediately after World War II. Soldiers returning from the war decided by the millions to "start a family." The annual birth rate nearly doubled for the next 18 years. Hence, the name, "Baby Boom", and "Baby Boomer".

I myself am an "alpha boomer", a first year Baby Boomer, born in 1946. I understand my generation. Yet, simultaneously, I am closer to the pre-boomer, pre-World War II generation than other younger Boomers. I understand the resistance to change that the older generation exhibits towards Boomers.

Boomers are the largest unreached people group in America because a majority of churches refuse to recognize them as the generational and cultural people group they undeniably are.

No other American generation had even a 10%, much less a 50% divorce rate. In the Pre-Boomer generation, people got married and stayed married. Then the divorce rate jumped to 50% in one generation. Guess which one it was? The Boomers!

Other simultaneous generational components of the Boomer-divorce generation? It was the first "TV generation," the first prosperity generation, the Watergate, Vietnam, Materialism generation.

After the Stock Market Crash in 1929, and the Great Depression in the years following, the parents of the Boomers said to themselves, "Nothing's too good for my kids. It's not going to be as hard for my kids as it was for me."

There are numerous books written about the Boomers. The best of these books is "Baby Boomerang", by Doug Murren. He pioneered a church for Boomers in Kirkland Washington, which now runs 3,000 to 4000 on Sunday mornings.

#7 Give New Testament scriptures for "targeting" specific people groups.

Did Jesus ever target people? Did He believe in "market research" and "marketing the church"? Did He believe in concepts like "receptivity and resistance"? Or, did He say, "Go reach everybody, everywhere, all at once, because all people are the same,"?

The same Lord Who said "Go preach the gospel to every creature," first told His disciples in Luke 10, "Do not go into the way of the Gentiles (or non-Jews), for I am sent only to the House of Israel."

Secondly, in Luke 10 and Matthew 10, Jesus instructed His disciples before sending them (the 12 and the 70), "When you enter a town, inquire or locate a house and man that is worthy." Jesus then defined "worthy" as "receptive" - those who would receive both the disciples and the Gospel they were preaching.

Jesus went on to say, "If they receive you, stay at their house. Do N-O-T go from house to house." He was educating His disciples in the concepts of "receptivity and resistance." Undeniably, He targeted them towards "receptivity".

He didn't send them to pick green fruit, nor to mangle or manipulate unripe "fruit" (people) they would also meet. With the unreceptives (or hostiles), Jesus instructed, "shake the dust from off of your feet."

Instead, He advised them to locate those that were receptive, and to center and base their Gospel-efforts through the web-friendship networks and homes of these same "receptives" (the King James here uses the word "worthy") interchangeably.

#8 Redemption, Lift and Isolation Syndrome

It is well established that the vast majority of Christians are most productive in reaching unsaved people before they reach the ripe old age of two years old in Christ.

Surveys say that the average Christian has either no (or very few) unsaved friends after becoming two years old in Christ. When we first get saved, we have mostly unsaved friends and few

Christian friends. Gradually, but continually, we become unintentionally isolated as we develop new friends in Christ.

First we get Redeemed, then we get blessed and "Lifted". By "lift", Donald McGavran writes in his masterpiece, "Understanding Church Growth", Christian values and ethics lift us out of degraded lifestyles into a new lifestyle, which rightfully creates new Christian friendships. Once Redemption and Lift take place, "Isolation" from the unsaved too often becomes the norm.

Soon, we go out after church for coffee and pie with Believers, we buy at Christian bookstores, and use the Christian Yellow Pages to shop at Christian-owned stores. Some even seek to drink milk from only "Christian cows".

A good strategy to overcome "R.L.& I Syndrome" is to link together New Converts, who have the most unsaved (Pre-Visitor) friends, with seasoned saints who are perhaps suffering from "R.L.&I.", but know God's Kingdom and God's Word better.

Chapter 12

The Three Paradigms

In 1958, the president of General Motors announced, "We've heard rumors about the Japanese automotive invasion of America. In Detroit, we're not worried about the Japanese because we, the 'Big Three' automakers, control the world automotive market, and always will. We have sixty models on the market, and say confidently the Japanese will never, ever gain any share of the U.S. automotive market."

Wrong!

Did the GM president have information? Answer, yes.

Did he sincerely believe his information? Again, yes.

Was he sincere in his statements? Of course!

However, let me ask: was his information accurate, current, and pro-active? Answer: unfortunately, no!

In 1992, General Motors posted its worst year in history, recording over $8 billion in losses, laying off 82,000 workers, and announcing the closing of twenty-three plants.

Whether GM's president in 1958 believed in the Japanese automotive "invasion" or not, nonetheless, it took place. Over the years, bit by bit, GM got out of touch with its customers. The U.S. consumer wanted better gas mileage and smaller cars, but GM was not listening.

The American customer wanted a quality product, rather than "planned obsolescence". Once again, GM wasn't listening.

How many readers want church leaders to be only as visionary as General Motors' president? We need more accuracy, and that requires constant information upgrading and updating.

The Tip-Off Word in the Phrase: Information Age

Contrary to the belief of some "hard heads", there is a tip-off word in the phrase, "the Information Age". A warm-up question might be, "What color were George Washington's four other gray horses?" Certainly, no one would doubt that with the age we live in titled as it is, the key word is "Information". Thus, we will need to use more information than at any previous time.

Let's look at some dimensions and components of these three major paradigms.

The Product

Obviously, the Agricultural and Industrial Age's products, respectively, were agricultural and industrial goods. But when we state that the main product of the Information Age is information and service, this leaves many people puzzled.

Information and data are increasingly the base of power, while providing service for the new support industries it spawns is the up and coming trend.

For example, the wealthiest man in America used to be Sam Walton (industrialist founder of Wal-Mart). However, now the richest man in America is Bill Gates, CEO and founder of Microsoft Software. At age 34, he is the youngest, and first 34-year old billionaire in U.S. history.

Service as a product? Fred Smith is a prime example. Before graduating from Harvard Business School, for his Master's thesis, he wrote a business plan proposing delivering of overnight mail.

His professor told him, "Good plan, Fred, but a non-viable idea. People neither need nor want that type of instant, overnight service." Wrong! Information Age people DO want "instant-just-about-everything". The success of Federal Express as a multi-billion dollar international company is the rest of the story.

Farmers in America

In the 1700's, 98% of Americans were farmers. The Industrial Revolution brought urbanization, and now less than 2% of the U.S. population farms for a living. Anyone nearsighted enough to train their kids to be small acreage farmers in this day and age (or for that matter, manual bowling alley pin-setters) is headed for future-shock.

The Distribution of the Product

Agricultural Age distribution was done with a horse and buggy or wagon. The Industrial Revolution introduced the iron-horse (Railroad) and the horseless-carriage (automobile). The computer is the horse and buggy of the Information Age.

Henry Ford introduced his first "Model T" in 1901, but forgot to put a reverse in the initial model. Ford is also known for the statement, "The customer can buy the Model T in any color he wants, as long as it is black."

General Motors came along and said, "If we want market-share, let's find out what the customers want and aren't getting." At its beginnings, GM did market research listening to potential customers, and discovered that people wanted cars in colors like yellow, red, white and blue, green, etc.

GM introduced the first cars in different color choices. By listening to customers, GM became the greatest multi-national automotive giant in world. Somewhere along the line, however, GM stopped listening and got out of touch with its customer.

I currently drive a Honda that was probably made in Kentucky. Millions of others like me in the U.S. every day are driving a Japanese car that GM's president said in 1958 would never happen.

The Japanese read the paradigm of the incipient Information Age (that the customer rules the market place), while "Industrial Age mentality" General Motors didn't want to change, and lost its way.

Forms of Money

In the Agricultural age, precious metals like gold doubloons, and silver coins were common. In the Industrial Revolution, paper currency replaced precious metals.

What is money's form today? Today's major money forms are plastic and electronic. Money is really now electronic blips and dots. In reality, it is binary code, 1's and 0's. These electronic symbols transfer globally in nanoseconds between governments, major banking houses, international stock exchanges, and the like.

Today, if one uses over $10,000 of paper money at a bank to buy a house, it may be perfectly good legal tender, but is the person respected... or suspected? Right! Suspected! In fact, the bank is legally bound to report it to the Federal government as a potential drug deal or money laundering. The reason: the person is massively "out of synch" (de-synchronized) from the current paradigm and realities.

Mobility

Agricultural age people traveled less than 200 miles in an average 35-year lifetime. In the Industrial Age, the railroad enabled people to cross the nation in less than a week, instead of months by ship or wagon train.

Now, in the Information Age, flying on a Supersonic Concorde, one can leave Europe at lunch time, and get to New York for breakfast the same day. You actually "arrive before you leave!"

The Mindset

In the day of the small, rural town, information took months to cross the nation. In the Industrial Age, information started to be telegraphed across the nation, informing people in minutes, what had previously had taken weeks and months.

Now, however, in the Information Age paradigm, people have a global mindset. Information travels globally in less time now than it used to take to go from one side of a small town to the other side of the same small town.

"Global village" is an ever-increasingly accurate description of the contemporary mindset. Churches must learn that "if you want to catch fish, you have to learn to think like the fish."

Percentage of Divorce

In the Agricultural age, divorce did not exist. The Industrial Revolution brought the gradual decay of family values, loyalty, and marriage. Now, however, divorces outnumber marriages in every major newspaper in the country. Over 1.4 million divorces take place each year - the majority of them among the Boomers.

Family Structure

Agricultural paradigm families lived in the same small rural towns for generations, and the "extended family" lived in close proximity. People had roots, and a sense of community.

The Industrial Revolution pulled the nuclear family to the cities, but entire, extended families did not make the journey. As a result downline, the nuclear family faced a slow disintegration.

Now, in the Information Age paradigm, the extended family is a memory, and the nuclear family is the exception. The 1990 U.S. Census reported that the standard nuclear family (Mom and Dad, two kids, first marriage) is now only 7% of the U.S. population. The nuclear family has been "nuked" and replaced by the fractured family.

In the 1950's, the average family had 3.2 kids. Today, the average kid has 3.2 parents.

Compare families like the Waltons (rural, extended family) and the Cleavers (the nuclear family of "Leave It To Beaver" TV fame in the 50's), to today's more normative representative family, The Simpsons - Bart, Homer, Marge and Maggie, etc. The only hope of the "nuked" nuclear family - and today's new fractured families - is the Church.

Respect for God

When America was founded in the Agricultural Age, respect for God, the Holy Bible, and the Church was high. The pilgrims at both Plymouth Rock and Jamestown risked their all coming here to worship the God of the Bible.

Religion increasingly lost its place of prominence with the demise of the extended family. Today, experts tell us America is headed toward becoming (or even worse, has already become) a "post-Christian" nation.

"Post-Christian" - the very words strike fear in the hearts of believers and cast a death-pall over the faces of most ministers. "Post-Christian" America! I hate to say it, and you hate to hear it, but if we don't wake up, what happened to Europe, bringing it down to being now only 2% Christian, will be our fate as well.

The Rate of Change

The Agricultural Age change factor was very, very slow. However, when one moves to the city (the essence of the Industrial Revolution paradigm), there comes a much higher frequency of change.

The Information Age "rate of change" has gone "ballistic". Today, we face not only regular change, but quantum change, change that can also be termed "toxic".

Futurists tell those with ears to hear that the change rate will accelerate ten times faster than that we have already experienced.

Question of the week: Date:

_____   _____

_____

- 1 2 3 4 5 6 7 8 9 10 +

Comments: _____

_____

_____

_____

**Actual card size is
4 x 6 - Feel free to
Xerox and use.**

Chapter 13

Question of the Week

In the Industrial Age, indoor plumbing, and hot and cold running water became standard. Any place without it was now judged by the new accepted standard, and considered primitive. Similarly, some new things have now become standard in the Information Age.

If most pastors and church boards were asked to describe an Information Age church, most would be hard-pressed to answer.

Obviously, an Information Age church must deal with the paradigm whose product and power-base is Information. Obviously, an Information Age church would have to deal with obtaining and processing a great deal more Information than ever before.

Although this seems like such a weak, auxiliary point, it really is a major key to successfully doing business for God in and beyond the 1990's.

Hot and Cold Running Information: The Why and The How

In the Industrial Revolution, people moved beyond the concept of running water in a nearby creek, or water pumped from a well, to that of water running in their house, right out of a faucet.

City dwellers grew used to the luxury of hot and cold running water. Soon, even the smaller, rural towns had running water, as well. Then they added the features of hot and cold running water.

Similarly, people of the Information Age (whom I affectionately call "Informationites") have grown used to the absolute necessity of having "HOT AND COLD RUNNING INFORMATION".

Included is a tactical information-gathering "stealth weapon" - a Question of the Week card to help your church install, operate, and continually benefit from "hot and cold running information".

Information age people expect indoor plumbing AND "hot and cold running information". A Boeing 727 cannot be powered by either kerosene or candle power, just as a kerosene lamp can't be powered by firewood. Both must be powered by the proper fuel.

Information Equals Power .

Information is the fuel of the Information Age.

Information equals power.

What plasma is to the body, "info" is to the new paradigm.

If we need more information in this new Information paradigm, where are we going to get it? We need good information, as well as bad; positive information as well as negative.

The Question of the Week card is normally a 4"x6" card. Seemingly of little potential, it is a tremendous "stealth" weapon.

Use this card to get at the information you're not currently receiving. "Information equals power" is the new paradigm formula for power. So get it flowing, and use it for God's Kingdom.

Does a church need more, or less, information about its community and Pre-Visitors? Correct answer - more.

What do people in your town think about your church?

What do new move-ins in your area seek most in a church?

Pre-Visitor information like this is helping growing churches grow. A lack of it is keeping plateaued churches from growing.

What do visitors want us to know that we're not asking?

Why are visitors coming once, and not returning?

Why do most visitors attend your church in the 1st place?

What makes your visitors comfortable...and uncomfortable?

What visitor-care improvements would your visitors like?

If Information equals power, then a lack of information will equal a lack of power. If you knew what your visitors are thinking, would your retention increase, or decrease?

Someone reading this may be saying to himself, "Yes, but that's secular market research." Response: Jesus said to follow Him, and He would teach us to fish for (and catch) the souls of men (Matthew 4:19). If you're gonna catch fish, you have to learn to think like the fish. What type of fish? "Filet of Soul!"

What information from your New Converts could improve your New Convert survival rate?

What information does your church not know about its New and Regular Members from which it might benefit? Who is going Inactive right now, even as this page is being read?

Information can assist just as radar assists a pilot in a storm.

Question of the Week: What Questions might you ask?

Questions that produce great insights into your Sunday morning congregation through individual Question of the Week cards:

(1) What are we doing well, and what are we not doing so well?

By asking this, you are asking for their help in reading their minds.

Of course, one can't read people's minds, but if you ask, they just might tell you.

(2) What sermon topics have we spoken on that you've liked most, and what topics would most interest your unsaved friends?

People like to know they're being listened to.

(3) What have we done for fun in the past, or could we do for fun in the future?

(4) What questions would you like to see asked of the church?

What church leader knows too much about his church, his congregation, their thinking, their likes and dislikes, dreams, hopes and fears?

This type of information is called "Psychographic" information and is much more powerful than at any time before.

What reader of this book will ever know too much about his church's attenders, potential attenders, Visitors, New Members, Regular Members, Inactives, and Drop Outs?

A Few Do's and Don't's in Using the "Question of The Week"

(1) Don't feel you have to do the Question of the Week every week.

Whenever you use it, it's the Question of the Week for THAT week. You DON'T want it to become routine or expected.

The congregation (and visitors) are impressed by any smart pastor getting fresh information (and "ammunition") for ministry.

(2) When you use it, you don't have to print separate cards.

Tell the people from the pulpit what the question is for that specific week. You can print these cards on 20 pound paper from a copy machine. You don't have to print the specific question on the card.

(3) Make sure you report back to the people some of your findings.

Let the people know selected bits of the information, high-lights, and a little bit of statistical crunch from the last Question of the Week. For example, what percentage said yes, what percentage said no, a few serendipity responses, a humorous or great creative thought. Share more "uppers" than "downers".

People dislike giving information (or volunteering) and then never being re-contacted. If you get a few negative responses, the great news is YOU DON'T HAVE TO SHARE THEM! However, most people will give victory reports or hilarious "one-liners", "silver bullets", etc.

(4) Remind people they don't have to put their name on their card.

You have to break the "code of silence" to get both "hot and cold information" running freely. "Hot Info" is positive news, while "Cold Info" is negative feedback. You need both kinds.

Most pastors think "bad news" travels fastest, but is the cliche' really true? Most pastors re-think the issue when asked, "Which is easier: for a church member to tell you face to face, 'Your sermon was fantastic!' or, 'Pastor, your sermons lately have been a bit flat,'? Obviously, good news (or "hot information") flows more freely.

None of us want conflict; thus too many things remain unspoken. They build up until one day...they EXPLODE! We need both "hot and cold" running information to let people "vent" and re-establish communication flow.

Chapter 14

Information Age Churches and "Cutting-Edge" Contacts

Following are ministries known for prototyping creative, innovative, and reproducible ministry in the Information Age.

Why not type a simple mailing list and materials/catalog request form letter, copy it and mail it to all listed below.

The rate of obsolescence in the Information Age is exponential. Only those that "cross-pollinate" and synthesize will stay on the cutting edge. Those that refuse to innovate and synthesize will be left behind like the dinosaurs.

Fuller Institute / Office of Continuing Education
1-800-999-9578
The International Center for Leadership Development & Evangelism
1-800-804-0777
www.fuller.edu/cll

Church Growth Inc.
Charles Arn
626-305-1280
1-800-553-4769

Barna Research Group
P.O. Box 4152
Glendale, CA. 91222-0152
1-818-241-9684

Elmer Towns
P.O. Box 4404
Lynchburg, VA. 24502
1-800-553-GROW

Carl George
P.O. Box 547
Diamond Bar, CA. 91765
1-909-396-6843

Pastor Bill Hybels
Willow Creek Community Church
67 W. Algonquin Rd.
S. Barrington, IL. 60010
1-847-765-5000 (write for cassette catalog)

Willow Creek Association
P.O. Box 3188
S. Barrington, IL. 60010
1-800-570-9812
www.willowcreek.com

North American Church Growth Society
% Fuller Seminary
135 N. Oakland Ave.
Pasadena, CA. 91182

Injoy Ministries - John Maxwell
P.O. Box 7700
Atlanta, GA. 30357
4725 Rivergreen Pkwy.
Duluth, GA. 30096
1-800-333-6506

Bob Logan Ministries
% Chuck Smart Resources
1-800-253-4276

Pastor Rick Warren
Saddleback Valley Community Church
1 Saddleback Parkway
Lake Forest, CA. 92630
1-949-609-8000
www.saddleback.com

Chapter 15

Willow Creek Community Church

One of the churches I admire most in America is Willow Creek Community Church (WCCC).

I admire its pastor, Bill Hybels. He, perhaps more than any other church leader in America, understands the current Information Age Pre-Visitor (Back Door #1), the section we are still examining. Before you crystallize an opinion about WCCC, go there. At least, read the following material. Don't allow jealous, misinformed, self-appointed critics to cause you to "throw the baby out with the bath water."

I've been to Willow Creek Community Church in South Barrington, Illinois (45 minutes northwest of Chicago) several times. I've attended all four "seeker services" on a given weekend. I've seen the 15,000 people come into the four weekend services. That's not bad for a church which is only 17 years old, and started from scratch with no backing.

Not bad for someone some "old timers" are convinced is doing "nothing right" and "everything wrong." Sounds almost like the Scribes and Pharisees of yester-year.

It reminds me of the young minister who asked one pastor why his church was declining and the reply came, "Because I'm being true to God, and preaching His Word."

The young minister went across town to ask a pastor of a fast-growing church why his church was growing and got the answer, "My church is growing because I'm being true to God, and preaching His Word."

Bill Hybels' turnaround came from "active-listening" and seeking input from his stagnant youth group. It grew from 30 to 1,200 in three years.

Does that give you any type of hint as to the accuracy of the new paradigm equation that "Information Equals Power"?

I'm not saying that's going to happen at every youth group in America, but allow me to share what did happen to Bill Hybels'.

As a youth pastor, his youth group wasn't growing, and the Holy Spirit spoke to him, saying, "Bill, things need to change."

Hybels responded appropriately by saying, "Speak Lord, I'm listening." He went to his youth group, and told them he knew some things needed to change. "I need your input. I want to see our youth group reach your high school for Jesus."

Improvement, by definition, requires change. Not all change produces growth, but all growth and improvement requires change.

If you and I are not changing, we're not only not growing, we're out of the will of God. The Bible says, "Be thou transformed by the renewing of your mind," (Romans 12:2).

Every church in America is feeling the heat of the paradigm shift. Most have "felt the heat," but have yet to "see the Light" of God's strategy for thriving, not just surviving, in the '90's.

Hybels felt the heat, and then saw the Light. He listened to his youth group. He asked, "What needs to change?" They said, "Bill you don't want to hear. It's probably gonna' hurt your feelings, and we don't want to do that."

Pastors, your churches are going to respond similarly to you as you set up systems to receive more "hot and cold running information".

You've got to CONVINCINGLY say back to them, "Write it anonymously if you like, but I've got to get at both the good and the bad. I really do want and need to know."

Hybels' kids said, "Well, Bill, first off, we need to change the music. We need a band, and some music about the Lord with a beat." Bill responded, "Okay, let's do it. Get electric guitars, drums, a bass player, but just keep the words Christian and understandable. Next, the kids said, "Bill, the carpet squares we sit on - they're too 'hokey'. We gotta' do better than that. The football captains, cheerleaders, etc. aren't gonna' go for that."

Bill replied, "That's okay, too. We can get chairs or benches, - no problem. Fine. What else needs to be changed?"

The kids continued, "Bill, we know you don't want to hear this one. We don't want to hurt your feelings. You love us, and we love you too. Maybe we better skip this one."

But Bill continued his "re-targeting" and said, "Whatever it is, tell me, IF it will help us reach your unsaved, unchurched friends at your high school who are headed for a 'Christ-less' eternity in hell without Jesus."

"Well, Bill, your preaching is good; we love it, but we're Christians. Bill, to reach our unsaved friends, you need to target relevant topics that young people will really be interested in, things from daily life, and daily struggles. Beyond this, Bill, your messages are TOO long! You need to preach shorter, more condensed messages to hold unsaved kids' attention."

***Editors Note: Sermons in churches reaching Baby Boomers are increasingly becoming shorter, aiming at a fifteen to twenty minute length. Some preachers would say, "Well, I need half that time just to warm up." Response: The Sermon on the Mount was eternal, but takes less than fifteen minutes to read aloud. The same is true for Psalm 119, the longest chapter in the Bible.

Which of these two choices do you prefer for your church?

Choice One: See your church go to two or three services by condensing your sermon length and see five times more true conversions by reducing your sermon length by two-thirds, or...

Option Two: Continue forty-five to sixty minute Sunday morning messages, "preaching to the choir", with less than a 1% unsaved visitor flow, and increasingly fewer true conversions?

****

Bill Hybels listened, and now Willow Creek is perhaps the most well-known church in America, perhaps second only to Cho's church in Korea.

WCCC has received free "advertisements" in the New York Times, USA Today, the Wall Street Journal, the London Times, Good Morning America, etc. Not just "free press", but free p-o-s-i-t-i-v-e advertising, saying good things in an increasingly negative post-Christian secular marketplace. Why? Because Hybels cared - and dared - enough to listen. He asked God for a fresh strategy to re-program and "hit the target" (his community), not just to continue dropping the bombs.

God answered His prayer. He longs to answer yours.

Bill Hybels goes door-to-door, listening to "the fish".

Bill went door to door in South Barrington (his community) for three months, eight hours a day, six days a week, before starting Willow Creek Community Church in 1975.

At each door he asked, "Do you currently go to church?" If they said yes, he politely proceeded to the next. He wanted to hear what the unchurched were saying. When he found the unchurched behind a door, he asked, "Why don't you go to church? We're just curious and really want to know why."

Question: Who knows more about the unchurched in your area - the churched, or the unchurched? That's right, the un-churched do. Hybels repeatedly encounterd these six recurring reasons unchurched people gave as to why they didn't like church.

In order of frequency, they were:
1. Churches were "always asking for money."
2. Unable to relate to the music.
3. Couldn't relate to the message.
4. The Church doesn't meet my needs.
5. Services are predictable.
6. The church makes me feel guilty.

Now you say, the Gospel is supposed to make people feel guilty. Isn't it supposed to do more than that? It's not a successful operation if you lose the patient.

In Luke 15:1 we read, "Then drew near to Jesus all the Publicans and sinners to listen." How many would like your church to be more "on-target", reaching and drawing unchurched people in your community. We need more precise targeting information.

Willow Creek Community Church continues listening and meeting real needs. Its one goal remains - to take unchurched people, and turn them into fully committed, devoted followers of Jesus Christ.

Chapter 16

Visitor Care Foundations

Next, let's look at Back Door #2, answering some primary questions dealing with Visitor-care and Visitor-retention.

What are some basic Visitor Assimilation ratios?

Both attracting and retaining more unchurched visitors are areas every church should seek to continually improve. Getting a numerical (or quantitative) handle on your church's "Visitor Flow" and "Visitor Retention" is crucial, and worth the required effort.

Visitor Flow: Those who have studied healthy churches (those averaging at least an annual net gain of 10% numerical growth) have determined a good visitor flow is five visitors per 100 Sunday morning worship attenders. These should be visitors from your local church "ministry area". Win and Charles Arn, in their classic "Church Growth Ratio Book" (see order form in back), state that visitor flow in plateaued churches usually runs two to three per 100, while churches in decline run a 1% or less visitor ratio.

Visitor Parking: This is another area that can be given a numerical handle as to an appropriate ratio. Since a church should have at least 5 visitors per 100 Sunday morning attenders, the desired number of visitor parking spots is easily attained by dividing that number of desired visitors by the number of visitors per car.

The number of visitors per car :

The number of visitors per car used to be 2.6 (or in the low three's.) That was when the nuclear family was normative in the 50's. Now, with over 50% of the American population single for the first time in U.S. history, using two as the number per car is easier, but probably a bit high. You may even want to divide by 1.5, or calculate more precisely your church's quotient by dividing your number of parking slots into your Sunday morning worship attendance.

Thus, a church running 300 on Sunday morning, should aim at a 5% visitor flow, or fifteen visitors. Dividing the fifteen visitors by two per car means the church should have 7 or 8 visitor parking spaces.

What are the two main types of visitors every church has?

At first this question seems simplistic. Every church has two main types of visitors - the saved, and the unsaved, those still "pre-Christian". I ask, "How different are the likes, dislikes and "worlds" of the saved and the unsaved?"

One might safely answer, "Different as night and day!"

Then why do most churches treat their saved and unsaved visitors exactly the same?

I am not advocating treating either group better or worse than the other. Don't instruct your ushers, "Ah, here comes a Believer. Seat him in the fancy pews, but oh! oh!, here comes an unsaved guy wearing Levi's and an earring. Better seat him in the back bleachers or back corner." No, not at all.

I am, however, saying that more specific, targeted treatment of the needs and responsive "hot-buttons" of each group will greatly profit any church's visitor-retention. Church visitors who are saved (or "churched") easily outnumber the "unchurched/ unsaved" by about 3:1, and probably much, much more.

George Barna tells us the average church shopper visits three to four churches one time each, with a "menu" of "felt-needs" and desires that he, she, or they are looking for.

The saved church shopper is a much more discriminating shopper, much more "menu driven". Knowing this, wouldn't it be beneficial to have an additional targeted packet for your church's "saved" visitors listing every ministry of the church in menu format, explaining in more depth the ministries that would appeal more to the "saved" visitors.

Keep these additional packets for the saved and churched instantly ready for greeters (and/or your Hospitality Team) to hand to "saved" visitors that openly announce they have just moved to town and are looking for a new church home.

Is there anything wrong or prejudicial in facilitating church-shoppers in finding their new church home at YOUR church?

Similarly, the unsaved have certain common, recurring needs. Why not have pre-selected literature that can be easily added to your standard visitor pack at the door to answer the questions commonly asked by the average unsaved person at your church.

What four things do visitors dislike the most?

Elmer Towns states that through repeated surveys, it has been proven that church visitors do not like to do four things: **"They don't want to stand up, speak up, sign up, or pay up."**

Despite numerous surveys proving these four points, some churches still insist on "urging" visitors do exactly these same four things.

At offering time, what does a world-class "seeker sensitive" pastor like Bill Hybels do at Willow Creek? He says, "We're going to receive the Lord's offering now, but if you're a visitor here today, you are our guest; this part of the service is not for you."

When one has a guest over to their home, they are welcomed in, and told, "Make yourself at home. What would you like to drink?" The host serves them, and makes them feel at home. Imagine a host saying, "That'll be 75 cents...plus Temple tax!"

Jesus understood how unsaved people think. He made people feel at home, and of course, He still does. Dare we aim or settle for any less?

What words are the most meaningful to visitors?

Visitors are impacted by words like "Wanted" and "Welcome." The outside of every Mormon facility has the same "visitor-friendly" message in large letters - "ALL VISITORS WELCOME" (see Luke 16:8).

If you don't go out of your way to make visitors feel comfortable, accepted, and loved, another church in town will. Just like mall shoppers, "church-shoppers" will "shop till they drop." They will "land" elsewhere when, with just a little more intentional welcoming effort, they would "land" at your church.

Define "Ethology" and apply it to visitor care and retention.

Ethology is the study of territorial, behavioral, and repetitive characteristics of living organisms. We are all creatures that operate with certain "pre-sets" towards territory and repetitive behavior.

When you go to a restaurant (or sit at a multiple session open-seating meeting), the next time you return to that place's main auditorium, you'll probably sit where you sat before. At a restaurant, you very likely menu-order the same item ordered before.

We are all definitely "creatures of habit".

Now let's apply these "ethological" characteristics to your church's visitors, who have these same characteristics.

Just as we are "habit forming" beings, the first time we do something or go somewhere new, our ethology is the thinnest, and least established during that crucial first visit.

If we bear this in mind, designing the most "visitor-friendly" entry-path for visitors at your church is the "smart thing" to do.

Contrast that to what a pastor told me happened at his church. Some choir members came down to the pews after singing the offertory. They approached some people in the pews who were first-time visitors and were overheard telling these newcomers, "Excuse me, you're going to have to move, these are our seats."

This of course made a great impression on these V-1's. What are the chances those V-1's ever became second-time visitors (V-2's)?

How can "visitor language" be updated and warmed up?

Sometimes, just a word or two can make all the difference. Language can be warm or cold. Language can be "warmed" up in many ways. Ushers can be called Greeters, Welcomers, or even re-titled as Hosts and Hostesses. The word "usher" sounds functional and institutional to many of the younger generation.

What does your church call it's visitors? Why not start calling them "Guests"? Which of the two phrases is more "high-touch", warmer, and more welcoming? When V-1's hear words like these, "If you're a visitor, you are our special guest here today. We want you to feel very much at home," - will it make them feel more or less wanted?

Another suggested change - your "Information Booth" can become your "Hospitality and Information Booth". Which word (or concept) is warmer - Hospitality or Information?

Hospitality in many churches is a lost, but recoverable, art. Could the ladies at most churches greatly improve the average level of hospitality given to visitors, if only given a leeway to do it? Without exception, I believe most men reading this would have to respond, "Yes."

Men have certain giftings, but I believe hospitality has some gender specifics to it, regarding the majority of the recipients the Holy Spirit has gifted with Hospitality.

When someone comes to a home, both men and women make an effort to help that person feel at home. Honestly, though, most wives can make people feel at home much more naturally than most guys.

We don't want just the male linear "event" dimension of welcoming visitors. We need to utilize as much of the total hospitality giftings God has given any congregation as is possible.

The Church Bulletin: At Harvest Church, we title the bulletin as our "Weekly Planner". This is a cultural thing. Boomers are into planners, Daytimers, and organizers, etc.

What words can be changed, warmed up, and updated at your church?

"Monday Evening Cookie Drops"

Our church policy is that every first-time visitor has a Hospitality Team drop off a nice plate of cookies the Monday night immediately following their initial church visit.

The Hospitality Team should leave the car running (except, of course, in "high crime" areas) and drop the cookies off, with a short but sweet, "We're Jim and Sue Smith from Harvest Church's Hospitality and Welcome Team. We're really glad you visited, and we hope you come back soon. Here's a little gift of some cookies and a bit more information about the church and its people-centered ministries. If we can help you in any way, or can answer any questions, please call on us. Hope to see you again this Sunday. Have a good evening. Bye!"

Don't stay an hour and interrupt their favorite TV show or major domestic argument of the week. Give an attractive, on-going relationship-building short contact.

Relationship building with the visitor is a process, and this "cookie drop" is a great first step foundation in the "getting to know one another" process.

Visitor Evaluation Cards: This is another great tool. When a church is open, teachable and creative enough to ask visitors to comment on what they liked and disliked, and how the visitor reception and main service could be improved, it speaks volumes.

One tip: Always include a stamp on the card, or use a pre-paid business reply device. Visitors will not pay the postage.

For a sample Visitor Critique Card, send a stamped self-addressed envelope to me, c/o Harvest Church, 9424 Big Horn Boulevard, #2B, Elk Grove, CA 95758.

As John Maxwell puts it, some of the most influential people in the entire church are the Ushers and Greeters. The first impression they make can determine whether a V-1 will ever "V-2".

Ushers can sometimes enter a "visitor blindness" mode, letting the power they have go to their head, rather than increase their serving sensitivity as doormen into God's Kingdom.

One Sunday, I was speaking at a multi-million dollar church. The ushers were huddled inside the door twenty to thirty minutes before service. It was a rainy day, and because I didn't have a 4x4 cross-country jeep, I had to park at the curb and carry a box of books in the rain about 75 feet to the door.

The "good old boy" ushers were talking to each other at the door, standing there, visiting, getting ready for their weekly "ushering and greeting thing". They clearly watched me walk the 75 feet of sidewalk in the rain without lifting a finger to help.

I was the guest speaker that morning, and they had several umbrellas hanging on hooks by the door. Yet not one had the creative "visitor-sensitivity" and unsolicited thoughtfulness to walk out and cover me with an umbrella while I walked in, having to use both hands to carry my box of books in the pouring rain.

Was I impressed by this team of ushers? You bet! I was

impressed enough to tell this story to thousands across the country, and to tens of thousands through this book and seminar.

What does a "low-touch" welcome like this do to the ethology and feelings of a first-time visitor? Contrast the way things might have happened with an improved "high-touch" scenario.

What if those same ushers had taken umbrellas, and walked out to greet and shelter me from the rain as I walked in? Does it matter who I was? What would a thoughtful welcome like that have said to me? It would have communicated, "We're glad you're here," and also, "What a creative and thoughtful group of ushers. "What an extra-thoughtful church," etc.

Umbrellas on a rainy day are a "stealth" idea. However, on a sunny day, they're a scud.

Further "State-of-the-Heart" Visitor Resources

"What Visitors See" is available through our ministry resources order form at the back of this book. This is a workbook with cassette from Carl George that will help in both curing (and preventing) "Visitor Blindness" at any church, including yours.

Chapter 17

George Barna's "Church-Shopping" Menus

George Barna, head of Barna Research, is the heir apparent to both George Gallup and Lou Harris, known worldwide for their Gallup and Harris Polls. Barna is the author of an increasing number of popular books including, "The Frog in the Kettle", "User Friendly Churches", and "The Power of Vision".

Barna tells us there are 80 million church shoppers in America. When shopping for a church, they will usually visit three or four churches, allocating one visit to each. The "church shopper" grades each church, and then compares "scorecards" or "report cards" kept on each church. They shop for churches with a "grocery list" in their mind, and sometimes even on paper. The visitor has usually determined before he leaves your church after his first visit whether he will ever return.

What would you suppose are the "most-wanted items" on their "shopping list"? Barna's first book, which the Billy Graham Association published, was titled, **"How to Find your Church"**. In its back appendix are four pages listing over 75 menu items that 1990's "menu-driven" church shoppers have on their "shopping-list".

For your benefit, I have copied a small portion of this grid. Buy the book, get the remaining pages of the grid, and review it with your board.

Action Item: Meet with your board and staff, discussing these menus and comparing information on your Pre-Visitors' "felt-needs" and visitors' "most-looked for" items. This would be a good item to write into your "idea-bank" page in the short-term column. If we're going to catch fish, we must learn to think like the fish.

Evaluation Criteria	Church name	Location	Date of visit	Church name	Location	Date of visit
A. Spiritual beliefs about:						
God						
Jesus Christ						
the Holy Spirit						
communion						
the Bible						
sin, Satan						
salvation						
sacraments						
purpose of life						
the role of women						
baptism						
spiritual gifts						
social issues						
B. Worship experience						
sermons						
music						
service contents						
style of worship						
participation						
tone of worship						
prayer						
attitude toward worship						

Chapter 18

A Great Seven-Step Hospitality System

Hospitality Introductions

Most people, when they come to a church, are greeted by the ushers. Some ushers greet them like this picture below. We call this, "Brother Doberman and Sister Rotweiler".

Of course, you don't have welcomers like that at your church, nor do we at Harvest, but some "other" churches come pretty close. There's even a California city called Growlersville - honest!

How "maximal" is the average greeting at your church? Every church has certain people they don't want a visitor to meet their first, second or third visit.

Brother Doberman

Sunday, 9:30 A.M., the elite visitor awareness commandos go into action.

Let's call the "Brother Doberman" welcome team Church A, and these "Visitor Awareness Commandoes" Church B. Which one are most churches in greater danger of resembling? Most readers will agree most churches are closer to Church A's welcome.

Since every church only gets one chance to make that crucial first impression, following are a number of specific, practical ideas to help your church put and keep its "best foot forward."

Hospitality Mentality

"Hospitality Mentality" is something every church needs to not only have, but constantly work on improving. Following is a "Seven-Step Hospitality" system to import as is, or customize and selectively implement as the Lord and your local church's needs and desires dictate.

High Tech - High Touch

One megatrend you absolutely must understand and apply is the concept of "High-Tech, High-Touch". This much misunderstood phrase does NOT mean to use "higher-tech" machinery to "high-touch" people. On the contrary, it means that as the technology gets higher and ever more complex, individuals increasingly feel more depersonalized.

To compensate for this depersonalization in their everyday world around them, people need to feel a much more intentional, more highly personalized "High Touch" treatment. Technology has exponentially increased, but unfortunately, most churches have kept their "touch level" the same for decades.

The friendly single handshake at the door that used to be a more than adequate greeting is no longer all that people need or expect. This operates on a subliminal level, by and large. People don't openly say, "Hey, I'm new at your church, my ethology is thin because I'm a 'V-1', so please give me lots of "High-Touch" to compensate for the depersonalized way the world treats me every day."

People don't say that, but they do think it...they feel it...they need it...and the churches where they will "land" and "stick" are those that will "High-Touch" them the best.

The technology curve, with micro-biology, nano-technology (with atom-sized machines to be loosed in the bloodstream to do operative procedures), "smart-insects", frost-resistant apples, mind-reading electro-encephalographic software, etc., means that the Church has got to catch up on its "high-touch" welcoming strategies.

To make fiberboard out of wood chips, one needs much more glue. Implications of this at your church are both widespread and eternal.

This takes us beyond the need, to the implementation and "how to" of a "Hospitality System" any church can customize and put into place.

Seven Step Hospitality Program and System

Hospitality Step #1:
Establish Visitor Parking

"Visitor Parking" should be as close to the main entrance(s) as possible. There should be signs directing visitors from their initial entrance into the church property all along the way. Visitor parking slots should also be visible from the front door by your Greeters.

The number of spaces should be basically two "visitor spaces" per 100 total Sunday morning attenders at your church. Thus, a church of 300 should have at least six designated, sign-marked "visitor parking" spaces.

Two additional high-touch "Parking Enhancement" ideas are:

Valet Parking for the handicapped, elderly, and single moms with kids. This is even BETTER than the usual reserved spaces for the elderly near your church entrance. It requires them to take fewer steps to enter the church, and frees close-up parking slots for visitors.

Umbrella Usher Teams on Rainy Days:

Is this a low-touch or high-touch idea? Why couldn't your church be the first in town to have "Umbrella Host/Greeter Teams" on rainy days - ESPECIALLY FOR FIRST, SECOND AND THIRD TIME VISITORS?!

Hospitality Step #2:
Hospitality and Information Booth

There are great benefits of having a Hospitality and Information Booth, staffed by an on-going Hospitality Team. Which is a warmer concept, the word "Hospitality" or "Information"?

Why not "warm up" the welcome, especially since you only get to make one first impression. Most churches greet their visitors with a smile and a handshake, give them a bulletin, and then the visitor socially "bungee dives".

What if a Hospitality Team at your church were strategically linked to your church's "Front Door Greeters"?

The process would go something like this:

A) The greeters "ID" visitors (from visitor parking slots);

B) Greeters alert Hospitality Team to V-1's approach;

C) As the Greeter welcomes the visitor, the Greeter casually "hands off" the visitor to the approaching Hospitality couple saying, "Well, Mr. Jones (the visitor), this is Steve and Sue from our Hospitality Team. Steve and Sue, this is Bill Jones and his wife Kathy. They've just moved to town."

Now, the Hospitality Team introduces themselves, continues the conversation between them and the visiting Joneses, slowly moving with them away from the front door towards the Hospitality Booth. This frees up the Door Greeter to continue welcoming incoming people.

To those who object to this highly intentionalized "entry path", let me ask: What DO you do for visitors A-F-T-E-R the greeter shakes their hand? And what could be done additionally?

Hospitality Step #3:
A Hospitality Center

Next is a Hospitality Center (or room) at your church. It should be near the lobby, but preferably NOT in it. However, even in a larger church, 100 feet away is too far away.

In some cases, the ushers may have to share their customary "hallowed special room" space as a Hospitality Center. Rather than start a "territorial" either-or war, find an acceptable compromise on that room's double usage. See Mark 9:23 and pray for a miracle!

Hospitality Step #4:
Hospitality Team Escorts

Hospitality Team Escorts stationed at the lobby Hospitality Booth can offer gently to A-C-C-O-M-P-A-N-Y visitors to the nursery, the hospitality area in the sanctuary, or allow them to "self-guide" if they so desire. **A domineering, insensitive escort is worse than none at all.**

Avoid telling visitors, "Here's a map listing Sunday School class options. Go down the hall 30 yards, take the second right, then the third left, up the stairs, and you'll find it. Nobody's ever gotten lost yet!" Low touch, or high touch?

Hospitality Step #5:
Between Sunday School and Worship Service

This is a "prime-time" hospitality slot. If a visitor doesn't know anyone at a church (or can't locate his friends) he sits alone in uncomfortable silence, twiddling his thumbs, re-reading the bulletin, etc. waiting for service to start. The Hospitality Center should be open and operative.

This is a time for "meeters" as well as "greeters".

"Meeters" are Hospitality Team members intentionally "hunting" for visitors. "Meeters" initiate conversation and extend an invitation to the Hospitality Center or designated church sanctuary Hospitality area.

Hospitality Step #6:
A Hospitality Area in the Sanctuary

What if there was a special area in the sanctuary that was designated and used as a hospitality area? This "doberman-free zone" would help concentrate and localize hospitality before and after each worship service. Even as a nursery needs to be kept "germ-free", you need a place visitors can "land" and receive maximal care and friendliness.

Hospitality Step #7:
Four After-Service Ideas to Consider

After service is the loneliest time for a first-time visitor. Here are a couple of ideas to enhance this after-service period.

After Service Idea #1: A Gift-Book for Every Visitor

At offering time, say, "If you're a visitor, you are our guest. This part of the service is not for you. We don't expect you to give to us. Instead, we're here to give to you. We have a gift book waiting for you at our front lobby Hospitality Booth. We have several titles to choose from which include, 'How to Make a Good Marriage Better', 'Building Healthy Relationships', 'Dads are For Spending Time With', 'One is a Whole Number', and 'Dealing with Disappointment with God'."

What does this gift book idea say to visitors? It says, "Hey, these people aren't takers, they're givers. I like that." It scores positive first-visit points.

After-Service Idea #2:
Hospitality Polaroid Photo Teams

(This idea is only for those who want more "young families" with children and more people in general to join their church.)

"After service at our Hospitality Booth, our Polaroid Hospitality Teams are ready to take a complimentary picture of you and whomever you came with. We'd like to take two quick photos. You may keep the one you like best as a memento of your visit. The other photo we'll keep and our prayer teams will pray this week for you to have the best week of your life." This is neither scary nor offensive.

Let me ask: do young families with children ever have too many family photos, especially all dressed in their "Sunday best"?

Now, your prayer team does pray over the photos. But what else is done? Over the next several weeks, that photo is reviewed on Sunday mornings before church by the greeters and the Hospitality Team on duty that week so they can recognize that visitor, perhaps even remembering the visitor's name.

This can also cut down on a common Greeter error: namely, asking a second or third time visitor, "Is this your first visit?"

The visitor replies out loud, "Well, no I was here the last two weeks also," but inside, his heart sinks and says, "Ah, nobody remembers me here. I guess I'm not that important or memorable to them."

Information equals what? P-O-W-E-R! Wouldn't this photo idea give increased visitor information to your greeters and hosts?

After Service Idea #3: Hospitality Dining Teams

Another "after-service" idea to announce from the pulpit (and print in visitor packs) is, "If you're a visitor today, every week a Hospitality Team family cooks extra portions of their favorite home-cooked meal. They would really like you (your family, or whoever you came with) to go home with them today and get to know each other. Most visitors won't take you up on that offer, but what does it say to the visitor about the church? That's right. "How thoughtful", "What a nice idea", "Maybe I'll take them up on that after another visit or two", or, "Hey, this is a friendly place."

After Service Idea #4: Weekly Visitor Reception

A brief reception for visitors to meet the staff and/or pastor after service, limited to pre-arranged select comments and perhaps a five minute introductory video, and accompanied by refreshments, is another idea to help diffuse after-service loneliness for visitors.

Morning service ends, Christians leave with family or friends, recharged with the love of Christ and the Word of God. However, the visitor walks up the aisle towards the exit, all alone.

Chapter 19

Newcomer's Class

What is the Ethological Development of First, Second and Third Time Visitors?

Experts like Win and Chip Arn have studied visitor retention (visitor "return rates") at many, many churches of different types and sizes. They state that in a church growing a minimum of 10% annually, the expected rate of return of first-time visitors is 25%; 50% for second time visitors; and 75% for third time visitors.

These are best-case scenario return-rates for churches that are "on the grow". For churches growing less than this, the retention rates are reduced. Unfortunately, most churches haven't the slightest idea of what their V-l, V-2, and V-3 retention rates are. It is their great loss, because it would greatly sensitize them to improving visitor-care policies.

The 25% V-l retention rate means that for every four visitors your church has, three will never come back.

A higher percentage of V-2's return than V-l's. This means 50% of second-time visitors may come back to your church. When you visit a church a second time, you're developing both a relationship and a habit. All people are relational, repetitive, and territorial.

When someone visits a third time, there is a 75% retention rate. That means that most of the V-3's (three out of four) will come back. When someone comes to your church a third time, they are in essence saying, "I like it here. I'm back. Do you remember me?"

If you can hold on to 75% of your third time visitors, wouldn't you want information about who is a V-1, V-2, and V-3 to help you preserve as great a harvest as possible?

Who are ethologically the most fragile of all church folk?

Ethology is the study of the repetitive, territorial, and habit-forming characteristics of people. Ethologically, the most fragile of all church-folk is the V-1. What do you do to soften and sweeten the "landing" of first-time visitors?

It takes thirty-two V-1's to create one V-4 (fourth time visitor) according to some estimates.

For every fourth-time visitor you have at your church, you've had to draw over thirty first-time visitors. Isn't it then imperative to do as good a job as possible with V-1's, V-2's and V-3's?

Can you define Newcomer Anxiety as related to your visitors?

Newcomer anxiety (or NCR Anxiety) is "new-turf nerves". When people are in (or entering) new territory, is their anxiety usually lower or higher? Higher anxiety, of course. This means people "spook" more easily. Once again, ethologically, a visitor's sensitivities are heightened and small things affect them more. Have you ever walked into a building for the first time, and missed a single step down that you didn't know was there? Remember how it "shook-up" your nerves for minutes after the event, or longer?

Every step must be clearly marked and thought-out for V-1's to avoid suffering the same thing in their emotions.

What percentage of those surveyed confessed to NCR Anxiety?

Fully 75% of those surveyed recognized the fact that they indeed were more anxious and had a heightened level of nervousness their first time at a new place. The other 25% were just "in denial" or out of touch with their feelings.

You know the feeling the first time you follow directions to someone's house. The second time you visit, the NCR anxiety level drops appreciably, doesn't it? The third time, you can almost drive there "in automatic", almost without the directions. Relate this situation to the newcomer/visitor and his first few visits.

Can you describe "Visitor Video Catnip"?

Allow me to explain the phrase, before applying it.

A cat-owner came into his living room one afternoon, to find his cat on the window sill, purring and "treading", growling softly, enchanted by the birds and squirrels on the nearby tree branches outside, so close, in living color, just beyond the glass.

The cat owner got a great idea! He ran and got his video camera. From out on the porch, he shot some footage fully utilizing the zoom lens. He used the editing mechanism in his video-cam, and a few days later popped the cassette into the VCR on his large screen TV. Next, he brought his cat into the living room, and pressed the VCR's play button.

The cat jumped up on the couch, started purring, meowing, doing the "tread", and growling softly. The cat liked what it saw IMMENSELY!! The cat started acting as if it was under the influence of catnip. Hence the name, "Video Catnip".

The man marketed the idea, and made himself thousands of dollars from the sales of duplicate copies of his innovative tape, which he marketed under the name of "Video Catnip".

Now apply the idea to the power of video and your church's visitors.

Undeniably, God is doing more wonderful things for more people in any given congregation than any pastor totally knows. These "victory reports" (highlights of people's lives, what God has done for them, benefits they received through their local church) are all magnetic, unbeatable advertising material.

What if you asked the question of your congregation, "What are the three things you like best about this church?" or, "How has this church changed your life for the better?" What if you then video-interviewed the people's responses after church some Sunday using several home video-cameras, perhaps tying it in with a church-wide potluck.

You would have more than ample great material to creatively excerpt out short "sound-bytes" of these positive comments of young couples, singles, teenagers, small children, grandparents, widowers, etc.

Combining these video-clip comments would provide a powerful, kaleidoscopic video piece about the benefits that YOUR church offers.

This is a powerful tool to give to first time visitors, whether as a loaner copy at your Hospitality booth, dropped off by your "V-1 Cookie Drop" visitation teams, or to show small portions of at your weekly after-church visitor reception as a powerful five-minute promotional piece.

Mix it down, and what have you got? Voila! "Visitor Video-Catnip".

Review some basic components of a Newcomer's Class and what it should include.

A Newcomer's Class is a designated "landing place" for the V-1, V-2, V-3 and beyond through V-8 or V-12. It should have a repeatable curriculum, and be the kind of class late-comers can merge into without disrupting a lecture, nor be embarrassed by having to walk up to the front row to find a place to sit down.

A Newcomer's Class should include such components as:

A. Wall-to-Wall hospitality and back row empty seats.

B. Two-way history-telling and weekly participation by **everyone** present. When the class exceeds ten or twelve, it is time to start another Newcomer's Class.

C. The class should have a preset- length, whether three or four weeks, eight or twelve, etc.) working on a rotating, on-going basis.

D. Have weekly "Visitor Video-Catnip" segments.

E. Activate Newcomer sponsors, adopters or friendship-teams.

F. Congregation members who bring friends should be encouraged to sit with their friends in the Newcomer's Class until it is completed.

G. Monthly Newcomer's Dinners (Newcomer's Night and off-site events) should be tied into the Newcomer's Class, and promoted for all the V-1's, V-2's, and V-3's during any given quarter.

Chapter 20

"V-2's": Second -Time Visitors

Cite the source and explain a "Seven Touch" Visitation program?

A great little book by Elmer Towns called "Winning the Winnable" has the elements of an integrated, well thought-out "Seven Touch" visitation program. Through this program, every visitor receives "seven touches" or contacts from the church before the end of the week after his or her first visit.

Explain Yeakley's "36-Hour Window"

Flavil Yeakley is an internationally recognized growth consultant, researcher and author. He surveyed those who do (and don't) return after their first visit to a church. He studied the church's visitation programs as related to "V-2" retention.

Yeakley found that if you will contact your first-time visitors within thirty-six hours of their initial visit, whether by phone, mail, or in person, 50% more of them will return, than if a church waits until later in the week, or beyond that.

It makes perfect sense.

When a visitor is contacted within thirty-six hours in a sensitive and friendly manner, it says to him or her, "These people really have their act together. They contacted me while my visit was still fresh in my mind. Maybe I'll check them out further, and see what else they've got going. I'm impressed!"

Conversely, what does it say to a visitor if he isn't contacted until two weeks, or a month later? It says just the opposite. The longer the delay, the more it insures the visitor will never return.

At Harvest Church, our policy has been that within the first thirty-six hours, every first-time visitor receives a letter, a phone call, and a cookie drop.

Can you relate the dynamics of digestion to V-1's, V-2's, and V-3's ?

Using the analogy of the human body, food DOES NOT DIGEST ITSELF. Instead, the body digests the food. In a church analogy, visitors don't assimilate themselves, rather the church (the Body of Christ) assimilates the visitor and helps make them a part.

Both Bob Logan and Carl George use this great one-liner, **"People go to church for a variety of reasons; they stay for primarily just one - relationships."**

The desire to belong and to be part of a family (or larger extended church family) is God-created.

The momentum and initiative, however, must come primarily from the church, not from the visitor. You must show newcomers that there is "room in the inn" for them, and that they are "VERY WANTED".

Now relate this to Jesus' statement regarding the Sabbath:

Food doesn't assimilate itself. Neither do church visitors assimilate themselves. In the old days, people were relationally healthy. They "digested" (or "assimilated") much easier than today.

Bulimia and Anorexia, which are really modern self-image "luxury" sicknesses, did not formerly exist. My Dad sold apples on the corner during the Depression. The only eating sickness he ever suffered was old-fashioned hunger: not having enough to eat.

Some people feel visitors should serve the church. However, this can get all turned around. Jesus said, "Is it right to do good on the Sabbath? God did not make man for the Sabbath, but the Sabbath for man."

Relate this to the Church. God did not make mankind for the Church (to serve the church). Instead, He made the Church to serve mankind.

When the Church (and its members) see themselves as God's hands and heart extended, to serve, love, win, and restore the visitor, the momentum is in the right direction.

However, when visitors start to represent increases in tithes and offerings to pay the bills, to fix the leak in the roof, to pave the next parking lot, or pay the power bill, "institutional self-preservation" becomes dominant and deadly.

Discuss what 'Name-Face recognition' and remembrance means to the repeat visitor.

If a visitor is remembered the following week when he returns as a V-2, he or she may give you "ten points". However, if a greeter somehow remembers their name and face, it gets the "gold ring", or 25 points of "bonding glue". We've already discussed how a Visitor Photo Team can help any church increase its visitor memory-bank.

Who intentionally monitors V-2 care at your church?

This is a vital area to jot down on the "idea-bank" page right now. Go over these items with church leadership and board. If your church doesn't have a Visitor-Care Task Force, start one.

What wouldn't make a V-l become a V-2 or V-3?

At the top of the list is the ultimate insult to a V-2: not being remembered. Also included in this list might be the inability to find a "menu list" of available ministries, or to make a "felt-need" known. A fourth item might be calling the church and not being responded to in a timely or appropriately sensitive manner.

Other Rentention Enhancing Resources include:

A. The book "Welcome" by Ervin Stutzman.
B. Three-cassette "Usher and Greeter Training Workbook" packet from John Maxwell's ministry (see order form).

Chapter 21

"V-3's": Third Time Visitors

It takes at least eleven V-1's to create one fourth-time visitor.

Here's the math:

Four V-1's create one V-2 (25% retention of V-1's).

Eight V-1's make one V-3 (V-2 retention is 50%).

V-3 retention is 75%. Thus, if eight V-1's create one V-3, then thirty-two V-1's will create four V-3's. Of these, at a 75% "stick-rate", a church will keep three of these V-3's to become three V-4's.

Divide the thirty-two V-1's by the three V-4's that are produced **and we see that it will take a minimum of eleven V-1's to create one fourth time visitor.** (The retention is much lower in non-growing churches.)

This means ten out of eleven V-1's never stick around long enough to become a V-4.

Percentage wise, 91% of V-1's (91 out of 100 first-time visitors), at even the highest retention churches, never become V-4's.

In reality, it takes many more V-1's, since very, very few churches keep 25% of their first-time visitors. If you keep one of eight, it will take twenty-two V-1's to create one V-4. And if you keep only one of twelve V-1's as a V-2, it would require thirty-three V-1's to retain one V-4.

If eleven, twenty-two or thirty-three people visit your church for every one that becomes a V-4, fine-tuning your visitor entry-path is obviously a vital element. No-one ever will become a member of a church that hasn't first become a V-l, V-2, and V-3.

What are V-3's saying to a church by visiting a third time?

By the third visit, a visitor has developed a habit and some "bonding" momentum. **In essence, a V-3 is saying to your church, "If you want me, you got me, IF you can keep up the same level of care and excellence in ministry."**

If the V-3 is saying this, what are they expecting to hear back from the church?

When people make a vulnerable statement like, "If you want me, you got me," obviously they want to hear back a solid, "Yes, we do want you, and we're really glad you're making the decision to become part of our church family."

However, since most churches don't know their V-3's from their V-l's, V-2's or V-22's, this crucial V-3 bonding statement is very often unheard and not responded to.

What happens when somebody becomes a V-3 at your church? What could happen, knowing now what you know?

What gift could be given to a V-3 to celebrate the third visit?

A pocket-size New Testament with the V-3's name engraved on it is a great, inexpensive gift. How about giving one to both the husband and wife, or perhaps, even to all the members of the family? This would be done from the church office after the third visit.

Obviously this is only for V-3's that live in the church's local ministry area, and who aren't currently attached to another local church.

Immediately, the cost factor rears its ugly head in some minds. May I ask two related questions:

Question 1: If a family of four (or even six) visits three times, and you give each of them pocket-size New Testaments with their names engraved on them, are they more likely to be more or less impressed towards becoming permanent members of such a loving church?

Question 2: If they do become a part of the church, going through New Member's class, and become faithful, tithing, members for the next five, ten or twenty years, will the $2.00 (or less) apiece invested in four engraved little New Testaments eventually be more than paid back? I think so! (Consult Galatians 6:7, 8 for details.)

Other V-3 recognition ideas might be:

A. A special quarterly (or even monthly) V-3 recognition dinner.

B. A special letter or handwritten note from the pastor(s).

C. A special congratulatory phone call from the Pastor and/or their Sunday School or Home Group leader, commending them on their third visit and encouraging them in the qualities and benefits of active local church membership.

With the third visit now an accomplished fact, the V-3 has developed a habit. Three out of four V-3's may return as a V-4. This is a great opportunity to invest visitation and care-ministries into a "target population" that will be highly responsive, rather than the one in one thousand (.001) success rate Mormons state they "catch" when "cold-calling" door-to-door.

Can you complete the phrase, "N- - groups for N- - people"

New people assimilate best in new groups. To assimilate new people into your church, you must continually start new groups.

It isn't a matter of going out and "killing" the older groups. Nonetheless, new groups are where new people with the fewest relationships in the church can - and WILL - intentionally go to find and develop the relationships they are looking for to meet their relational needs. This is where they will bond with your church. We'll study this further under Back Door #5: Regular Members.

Sunday morning's larger worship service is not the place to develop relationships; small groups and off-site events are. New-comer receptions, desserts, Newcomer focus groups, etc. are more productive for this.

What top three things stop V-2's from ever re-visiting the church for the third and pivotal visit?

As previously mentioned, not being remembered tops the list. Beyond that, they include not being able to express one's specific "felt-need" or not being given a menu of available ministries at that church.

How do visitors make "felt-needs" known to staff at your church, beyond what - for an increasing number - is the embarrass-ment of walking forward at an altar call?

A third thing might be not receiving enough Vitamin "C.A.L." (Comfortable, Accepted, and Loved).

How does your church intentionally help its V-3's answer the all important question for them - "Am I wanted, am I needed?"

Since many are inwardly asking that question, how does your church answer?

How are too many churches today operating in the Information Age almost as "Restaurants without a menu?"

How do V-1's, V-2's and V-3's find a menu of all available ministries at your church, or for that matter, at most churches?

Since the average Church Shopper will visit four churches (each one only once), wouldn't a paradigm-wise Information Age church make as much information available as possible on the crucial first visit?

Do you have a "menu" in print of all the available ministries at your church? Living in a "menu-driven" society, with "menu-shopping" visitors, shouldn't more churches think this way?

Restaurants without a menu:

If a restaurant didn't have a menu, would you even stay to eat? You would probably say, "These people are so far off the norm, their hygiene and food preparation are probably also "off the wall."

Or, envision with me, a restaurant menu with large subheadings such as Appetizers, then blank space, then Salads, then Entrees, blank space, then Desserts, then Beverages, etc.

You tell the waiter, "Okay, for an entree, I would like roast beef. Do you have it tonight?" The waiter laughs and says, "Ah! Fooled ya! No roast beef. Guess again!"

How many times would you guess before you would walk out. Today's Information Age people (the "Informationites") want information, and they want it when? They, (meaning WE) want it NOW!

We want the information... and we want it now!

Anymore, it is insufficient just to say, "We have Men's Ministry, Women's Ministry, and Children's Ministry. That's like saying, "We have ceilings, floors, walls, running water, and indoor plumbing." We must be more specific.

What type of Women's Ministry?
- Is there something for working women that meets on Saturdays?
- Is there a single moms' group?
- How about a M.O.P.'s (Mothers of Pre-Schoolers) group?
- Special women's speaker events?
- Charity events and support networks for single moms?
- A group for wives of unsaved husbands? (At Harvest Church that group is called "Beloved Unbelievers".)

People need and want more specific information.

And when they want it, they want it when?

Right!

Chapter 22

Questions for Your Visitors and Visitor Care Policies

When we ask better questions, we'll get better answers. The saying, "If you want to catch fish, learn to think like the fish," was never more true than in the current Information Age.

At the end of each section covering one of the Seven Back Doors will be a page of questions to ask and... for which to obtain answers.

Many questions regarding visitor likes and dislikes can be asked and answered through a postage-paid Visitor critique/questionnaire.

Since "Information Equals Power", learning all you can about your visitors' likes and dislikes is vital. This is called "psychographic information". A key part in Bill Hybel's success is prayer and the information God directed him - IN PRAYER- to find out so he could know all about those he was trying to reach.

Following are some questions to help your church ask and get the information it needs about its V-1's, V-2's and V-3's.

Questions to Ask Your Church's Visitors

1) What main things did you like most at our service?
2) During Worship service, what made you uncomfortable?
3) How would you improve our Visitor-Care systems?
4) Would you attend a ten-minute Visitors' Reception after either the first, second or third time you attended our church?
5) Will you return to our church? Why or why not?

Questions to ask of Your Visitor-Care Policies

1. Do we have (need) an ongoing Visitor Care Task Force?
2. Are we getting specific and timely information on who our V-1's, V-2's and V-3's are?
3. Is there room for improvement in our Visitor Care?
4. Where do most of our Visitors come from, and why?
5. Do we have a healthy or unhealthy "visitor-flow" ratio on Sunday mornings?
6. How does our congregation feel about inviting their unsaved friends to our Sunday morning services?
7. What would encourage more of our church to invite and bring their unsaved friends to church on Sunday mornings?

Chapter 23

New Converts Introductions

In John 15 verses 8, 16, Our Lord Jesus said, "In this is My Father glorified, that you bear much fruit, and that your fruit remain."

What can be learned to win the Back Door War regarding the loss of New Converts so prevalent in churches today?

How much can a newborn baby care for itself?

The answer is "not at all". A new baby can do nothing to care for itself - nothing! It is 100% care-dependent and helpless.

How does male dominance relate to New Convert survival and care?

Male-dominance in the American church is commonplace. Being one (a male), I can say with total objectivity that males do have many good character traits. I am also thankful for my wife and the other ladies (my three daughters age 20, 17 and 20 months) in my home.

Males and females think differently (as if you hadn't noticed).

Men are more linear thinkers. They are heavier users of the left-lobe of their brains, whereas women are more right-lobed, or relational, process thinkers.

Gary Smalley tells this great story on his marriage video tapes. When on a family vacation, driving 400 miles to Lake Wherever-you-go, the family finally piles into the car and gets on the road. After several hours on the road, the kids are fussing in the car. The wife says, "Honey, let's stop at a rest area. We've driven a good bit now. The kids need to let off some energy; they're driving me crazy. Can't we stop, Honey? Is there any good reason?"

The typical male replies, "Well honey," and then pauses, as he tries to come up with an excuse for not stopping. We dare not verbalize what we're thinking in our hearts, which is, "Honey, if we stop, all those cars we passed on the highway are going to pass us and get ahead of us."

That is linear thinking. Males are linear and think "the bottom line". When we're on a trip, what we want to do is to GET THERE!! We are much more "event", rather than "process" oriented. The wife is thinking, "Let's just enjoy the journey" (the process), but the man is thinking, "Let's get there" (the event).

"Fifty-four converts last year at Easter."

I once asked a pastor, "How was your Easter outreach last year?"

He replied, "We had 54 converts come forward."

"That's wonderful," I replied. "How many of them are still active or involved with your church now almost a year later?"

He responded, "To be honest with you, I'm not sure if any of them are." He then continued on with the conversation, jumping to another subject, without skipping a beat.

This is definitely male, linear, non-relational thinking. It does not speak well for New Convert survival and the nurturing, "feeding and folding" process, when there is an overly linear, male emphasis on the altar call (as a one-time event).

"Over 400 converts just last year alone!"

I spoke with another pastor who said his church had over 400 converts last year. I asked how many of them were still active in his church. He consulted with his staff, and came back with a figure of about 5%.

Why is the USA only 22nd best globally in Infant Mortality Rate?

Why does the USA, with its world-leading medical technology, have a rate of 9.8 deaths per 1,000 - double the world's lowest rate in Japan of only 4.8 deaths per 1,000?

In part, the blame goes to an overly male-dominated medical establishment that is too "linear". There are doctors who have to get to a golf game, tennis or racket ball match. If baby isn't born by such and such a time, they often take it by Caesarian.

Every other nation in the world with lower infant mortality rates is more midwife dependent, readier to wait out the natural process.

How many diapers does a baby use in one year? Relate to convert care.

Diaper service in California is currently about seventy diapers per week. Multiplied by fifty-two weeks per year, that's over 3,500 diapers - 3,640 a year, to be exact. Now multiply that number by the two and a half to three years to "potty-train", and that's about 10,000 diapers per child.

It takes a lot of care and pampering to bring up a newborn baby to that "D-Day" (day of diaper liberation).

Give some scriptures for New Convert Sponsor Teams?

When Saul (or Paul) was a new Christian, his church-persecuting past separated him from the support of the Jerusalem elders. It was Barnabas who sheltered him and brought him into favor with the elders, nurturing him, vouching for him, teaching him, etc.

The book of Philemon relates the story of Onesimus, a slave who had run away from his owner, Philemon. Paul had recently led Onesimus to the Lord, as a New Convert. Being a New Convert sponsor for Onesimus, Paul entreated the slave's owner Philemon to receive the New Convert runaway not harshly, but as a brother.

Ultimately, Jesus Himself is our eternal Sponsor and Advocate. He carries us, teaches us to crawl, then walk the Christian walk, one faltering step at a time.

How many times have we fallen, and Jesus has gently picked us up and set us back on the path with the words, "I know you can make it. Let's get back up, and try it again.

What seven factors increase New Convert retention and survival percentages, according to surveys by Flavil Yeakley?

Many of the following factors reveal a reversal of the old formula, "Win them, then assimilate them.

Churches are increasingly finding in the 1990's that the above formula works better in reverse of its former self, meaning, "**First Assimilate them, then win them**. Then, they will "bond to the local church that wins them, and become "fruit that remains.

The Seven High Retention Convert Factors are:

1. They received a witness (or more than one) from a friend.
2. They received the Gospel through multiple hearings.
3. They received a non-manipulative presentation in a dialogue format rather than a one-way monologue presentation.
4. High retention converts usually had a pre-existence of multiple friends in the church before the point of conversion.
5. The lower the pressure for an immediate decision, the higher the retention rate in the longer run.
6. The more dissatisfied they were with their lifestyle before conversion, the higher their retention rate after conversion. Converts who "stick were dissatisfied with their prior lifestyle to the point of being willing to embrace a serious life-change to get beyond the 'Is this is all there is?' barrier."
7. The higher the number (and greater the intensity) of major Life-Change factors (and major "stressors) active in their life right before conversion, the higher the retention rate.

What do High Convert-Retention Rate churches do differently?

The survival of New Converts is of primary importance to churches that produce a higher percentage of "fruit that remains. Many of these churches would rather have 100 converts yearly and keep 75 of them, then have a 1,000 convert total, and have 950 unaccounted for at year's end.

Additionally, many of these churches won't pray with potential converts who are at the point of conversion without including the importance of the local church.

Thus, unless converts commit to being part of "the" (or at

least, "a") local church, they won't proceed any further in prayer.

"High convert-retention" churches also stress the indispensability of an intentional "nurture phase" in all of their evangelism program and worship service opportunities to receive Christ.

God does not birth babies to let them be abandoned and die out in a field. Every week in America, 1,000 babies are abandoned on doorsteps. What tragic consequences await churches who treat carelessly the eternal fruit God has entrusted into their keeping. Surely there will be a day of accounting for the lives of the spiritual babies born into each congregation.

Other creative New Convert care ideas and resources include:

A. A good, New Convert class on audiotape from Pastor John Maxwell's Skyline Wesleyan Church.

B. From Pastor Rick Warren and Saddleback Community Church, a good basic New Convert class on audio tape.

C. LLI (Lay Leadership Institute) has a great conversion/ altar piece called "Congratulations! Some of its benefits include the fact that it contains three mini-Bible studies (three or four short questions each) in it. Thus, the altar worker can review the first three-question study, and then ask the convert to call or meet again to finish the next mini-study in the next day, two or three.

Chapter 24

New Convert Nurture

Undeniably, there are numerous similarities between new-born natural human babies, and newborn spiritual babes in God's Kingdom.

A. Both kinds of babies are tremendous blessings.

B. They both require a tremendous amount of work and care.

C. Both do absolutely nothing for themselves.

If you expect your New Converts to do anything for themselves, forget it. Unless a church is going to spoon-feed them according to I Peter 2:2, "As a newborn baby, desire the sincere milk of the Word," they will die long before their first spiritual birthday.

Let me illustrate this extremely high "D.Q ("Dependence Quotient) by the following analogy.

What is the Achilles' Heel of most New Convert Classes?

Is it the teacher who usually fails to show up, or is it someone else who is usually missing? Heavy rhetorical question!

Of course, the ones usually missing from New Convert classes are the "babes in Christ themselves. The expectation is that the New Convert, if sincerely converted, will somehow just "show up at New Convert class.

However, in real life, if you want a newborn baby to be somewhere at a set point in time, you can't just send an invitation. What do you have to do?

Right! **You have to BRING them if you want them there!**

Describe God's Sponsorship Program and New Convert Analogies

In God's divine order, in the natural realm, regarding procreation of new life, God set up the institution of marriage, to provide a sponsorship team of a husband and wife committed to each other.

Then, and only then, does God's divine order allow men and women to partake in the joys (and responsibilities)of procreation.

God's plan eliminates children being born without committed parents to provide protection, provision, and upbringing.

God's Divine order states: NO SPONSORS: NO BABIES !

God's plan never included babies being born unwanted, nor tragic abortions supposedly "necessitated" by the lack of sponsorship rather than by direct disobedience of God's commands.

The abortion Holocaust, (now numbering 1.5 million per year): 20 million in the USA alone since the 1972 Roe V. Wade Decision) was never part of God's plan for man.

How many spiritual abortions take place each year among America's 330,000 churches because of a lack of pre-planned convert sponsorship teams?

God clearly commands: Commit to each other and get married for life first, then you get to enjoy both sex, and procreation's benefits."

God's formula is: NO SPONSORS.... NO BABIES !

However, in most churches, what is the usual situation with "babes in Christ"(New Converts)? You got it.

Continually, there are too many babies, never enough sponsors.

The situation MUST be turned around. God's wisdom foresaw that a baby couldn't survive without intentionalized, highly committed, pre-arranged sponsors and "nurture-care".

God didn't leave 'child sponsorship' to ONE sponsor, but to two. Wise churches would do well to copy God's Divine sponsor plan.

3 : Discuss Pickett's discovery regarding Convert survival and motives.

Bishop Waskom Picket discovered through massive research on New Convert survival that "after-care" greatly outweighs the convert's original motive. Aftercare (or nurturing) is far more important than motive. Aftercare is followup: the "feeding and folding" of the baby.

What do most churches do when a convert fails to 'stick" and grow? We've heard it over and over. Too many churches blame the convert, instead of examining their `aftercare'. The usual rhetoric (and thought) goes like this : " Oh, well, if they were truly converted, they would have made it through, bonded, and become mature disciples."

This once again, is overly-dominant, male, linear thinking, rather than a healthy balance with relational, process thought.

#4: Let me prove the "Convert-motive" vs. "Aftercare" case:

Ask yourself: Which of two babies is more likely to survive? A healthy, full term nine pound baby (analogy, purest motive) with no aftercare, or a 3 month premature baby born at 5 1/2 pounds, given 24 hour, intensive-care-unit tending and care?

Doesn't this make sense? The unhealthy baby (or inferior motive convert) with superior aftercare and nurturing will (in the longer run) do better than the healthy baby with no care.

If a baby gets sick and dies, whose is the primary responsibility? Is the baby at fault? We all know the answer.

Mom and Dad are the primary ones responsible to make sure the helpless infant survives and is properly cared for.

"Convert-mortality" cause (and blame,) needs to be correctly traced . . . and replaced . . . if it is to be eliminated.

#5: Define "failure to thrive" syndrome and relate to convert care?

"Failure to Thrive" syndrome is a proven physiological phenomenon that has been documented, and is now intentionally prevented from occurring in hospitals everywhere.

In "Failure to thrive" syndrome, a baby's vital signs drop until the baby dies, even though it has a perfect environment (temperature, feedings, enough liquids, perfect hygiene, diapers changed, etc.).

The baby dies from "Failure to Thrive" UNLESS it feels loved, UNLESS it feels wanted ,and is adequately, regularly touched, and hugged. The emotional needs of the baby override the mere physical dimension. An unloved, untouched, and unheld baby wastes away. Feed it all you want, it will still die. How many New Converts die of "Failure to thrive" in your town?

#6 Name Lay Literature International's Four Phases of the Great Commission? Identify the phase most lacking in convert care?

A) **LLI's 4 phases divide the Great Commission into:**
   1) Evangelism
   2) Nurturing
   3) Discipleship
   4) Mobilization into Ministry
B) **The phase most obviously lacking in American church convert-care is the "nurturing" phase.**
   1) Evangelism: Yes, we believe in that.
   2) Nurturing: Ah well, we roll this into Discipleship.

3) Discipleship: We believe in that, so much, that we say (through our policies) to a newborn babe: "stand up and be a man"

4) Mobilizing believers into Ministry : We tell believers there is plenty of work to be done. "Don't just stand there, do something", we tell them. But as far as systematic mobilization of church members, according to their spiritual gift, ah well. "We'll cover this under "Back Door #5" later in this book."

The crucial step missing between Evangelism and Discipleship is nurturing, bringing New Converts to and through toddlerhood.

#7 Discuss the phrase "high impact, low maintenance" converts:

A leading evangelist has a book out that proudly states: "what we need are more `high-impact, low-maintenance' converts."

Pure fantasy. Rubbish! There is no such thing as a `high-impact, low-maintenance' baby, either in the spirit or the natural.

Now "high-impact" babies are commonplace. EVERY baby is "high-impact", as far as the Impact for "high-care" and "babying".(Just ask the Mother) A "low-maintenance" baby? Come on! Linear thinking once again.

#8: Discuss gender strengths in the area of nurture and "after-care"?

Nurturing is something that God Himself puts in the heart of a woman. Nurturing, (even more than the spiritual gift of Hospitality), is a largely gender-specific gift.

"Mother-love"(between a Mom and baby) is something men do NOT possess. Yes, we men have "father-love", and yes, we love our babies and children just as much as our wives do.

But linear, event oriented, "bottom-line" male thinking is NOT the nurturing, ongoing relational, emotional "umbilical cord" that God gives Moms. Nurture is a female-gender dominant gift.

#9 : What elements should Convert Sponsor (and Nurture) Teams Have?

A) New Convert Sponsors should be "non-maxed", not even close to the "burnout" or flash point.

B) Sponsors should be as close to an "affinity match" as possible. By "affinity", I mean, similar life-stage, experiences, background, interests, hobbies, etc. The statement "Ministry flows best where Affinity exists" is a powerful guideline for trying to find Convert Sponsor (and New Member Sponsor) compatibility.

Who can better relate to a single Mom, than another (or former) Single Mom. Who better relates to a teen, a widower, a blended family couple, etc. than someone who is, (or has been), where they are.

Chapter 25

Questions to ask New Converts and Your New Convert Policies:

Remember, when we ask better questions, we will get better answers.

1) Questions to ask New Converts

1) What do Converts who survived attribute their survival to?
2) What do your church's New Converts wish the church would both implement (and/or eliminate) in the New Convert care?
3) What do converts that "didn't stick" have to say to phone interviewers about what the church should/could have done?
4) What characteristics are there in common among the New Converts at your church that did stick,"survive" and thrive?

Questions to ask your New Convert care policies?

1) In the past year how many converts has your church birthed?
2) Does your church have a 'New Convert Care' Task Force?
3) What is the one-year convert survival retention percentage?
4) Are your church's Convert Care policies written down?
5) What are other churches in your town doing to improve their Convert Care, and Convert survival rates?
6) Would a Convert Sponsor program help more converts make it to and through the one year survival barrier?

Chapter 26

Back Door #4:
New Member Intros

Each of the seven back doors has its own idiosyncracies, individual problems and solutions. What about Winning the Backdoor War dealing with New Members. We will use the code for New Members, NM extensively once again.

Just by way of review, the codes for the seven back doors are: P-V (Pre-Visitors), V-1,2,3 (Visitors), NC (New Converts), NM (New Members), RM (Regular Members), IA (Inactives) and DO (Dropouts). Following, then, on the next eighteen pages is a synthesis of the best strategies for developing and preserving New Members.

#1 : What are four main reasons for low New Member Recruitment.

A. **<u>Over-spiritualizing and under-intentionalizing.</u>** Many churches relegate the entire New Member process, (from recruitment to preservation,) to the "sovereignty of God", things that God has clearly called them to do W-I-T-H His help. A farmer can (and should) pray all he wants, but if he sows little seed, Galatians 6:7,8 says he'll reap little harvest.

B. **<u>Lack of Seeding:</u>** Often churches have either too few or no New Member brunches, testimonies, recruitment events, etc. Then, they wonder why they produce so few New Members.

C. **No Ongoing Pastor's Class:** Ecclesiastes chapter 1:7 puts it, "All the rivers run into the sea, and yet the sea is not full." If a river's tributaries and creeks don't flow into the streams, and the streams feed into the river's main course, there would be no river. We must continually ask: What tributaries flow into and feed the New Member processes at our church?

D) **No Regular, Ongoing New Member Class:** Many churches have no regularly scheduled, New Member Class at their church. The class should be ongoing, intentionalized, and taught from a written formatted "curriculum", so it can qualify, train, and create New Members.

#2 How dangerous is the myth: Joining & belonging are synonymous?

This is perhaps the #1 mistake made by churches dealing with their New Members. This assumption passively underlies haphazard New Member assimilation, causing it to be unintentionally "left to chance".

If it is imagined that a New Member automatically attains a sense of belonging, logic would preclude any monitoring or intentional enriching of this dynamic. This helps a church "let down its defenses" as to New Member loss, since assumptions are lined up towards the "J = B" "magic formula: joining equals belonging." Thus , NM loss takes place mainly unnoticed.

3: What percentage of New Members drop out in the first year?

The common statistic/percentage given is that 50% of New Members drop out of their churches within the first 12 months after joining. This period is called the "at risk period", and should be closely monitored by churches desirous of keeping their New Members through this perilous initial bonding period.

Obviously, no one ever becomes a Regular Member, that doesn't first become a New Member and survives this first year "at risk" period. What does your church intentionally do to help its New Members make it through the first 365 days of Membership?

4: Illustrate & explain) the "Background Theory" and its vital ramifications in (and for) any congregation.

Below is a diagram of the Background Theory and its basic components: two concentric circles, an inner one and an outer one. **You must read Lyle Schaller's book, "Assimilating New Members" from which this is excerpted to get the full treatment on this and many, many other vital, related assimilation concepts.**

The Inner circle is the Fellowship Circle and represents those who feel they truly "belong" to the church they have joined.

The outer circle is the Membership Circle and represents those that have officially joined the church, but somehow they still don't feel they've really been accepted and that they really belong.

Benefits of doing a church-wide Background-Theory survey:

No pastor can read his people's minds. It used to be that no one could see any further than the natural eye. Now, of course, telescopes, binoculars, and even infra-red night scopes help SWAT teams and soldiers see great distances even at night. There is radar to be able to see through fog and clouds.

A "Background Theory" survey of your church's New Members, at the three month interval after they join, would provide valuable data as to what proportion of NM's truly feel they belong, or don't.

A church might mail survey cards out to all your New Members by name, briefly but clearly explaining what the two circles mean, and asking them to ANONYMOUSLY use the stamped self-addressed envelope placing their `x' wherever they feel they are in relationship to joining and belonging, whether in the inner circle of the church, between the two circles, or even outside of both.

5: What happens if people don't feel they belong?

People such as New Members feel they've done all they can to "belong". If such people don't gain the feeling that they belong . . . before too long . . . they're going to say "so long".

People will not commonly tell you they're not bonding, not making friends, or not feeling at home. They save it all up, and then one day, wham . . . they're gone!

A good analogy is divorce. Divorces don't happen over one night. They are an accumulation of weeks, months, and years of non-communication, relational-starvation, and "unresolved conflict". One day it reaches explosion level, and implodes!

#6 : What is the basic ratio discovered regarding friendships and New Member retention?

Chip Arn in "Church Growth Ratio Book" states (and explains why) every New Member should have developed a minimum of seven friendships within the first six months after joining.

Surveys of Inactive New Members (the 50% that don't make it through the critical first year after joining) revealed a common thread, namely that 85 % of Inactive New Members stated they had developed three or less friendships at their church.

Conversely, 90% of active New Members reported they had developed a minimum of 6 new friends or more during that same crucial six month time period.

#7 Explain the concepts of 'gatekeepers' and 'sponsors'.

In the story of Joseph in the book of Genesis, Joseph's brothers were prototypes of the customary, average "gatekeepers." Gatekeepers are those self-appointed 'screeners" of new ideas, newcomers, and New Members in particular, who say, in a thousand different subtle and openly hostile ways, " We like you, You're in" . . . or "We don't like your kind . . . move on down the road."

I call Joseph's brothers (in Genesis) the "Smother's Brothers". Joseph's brothers tried to smother his dreams. David's brothers were similar in their heart attitudes. In Matthew 23, verse 13, 14, Jesus said to the Pharisees and the Scribes, "You stand in the doorway to the Kingdom of Heaven. You won't enter yourselves, neither will you allow those who want entrance, to come in." They were self-appointed "road-hogs", blocking the way for people trying to get into God's eternal Kingdom.

Which gatekeepers (if any) keep people from entering your church? In what ways do they operate, and what should be done about it, both in the "now", and to prevent recurrence?

Chapter 27

New Member Class

Before people become New Members of your church, what have they been exposed to regarding church membership. What are the expectations? What should New Members be taught, shown, qualified by, exposed to, informed of, committed to? This is obviously the purpose for the New Member Class. Below are some vital elements.

#1: Seven Key Elements a New Member class Should Include Are:

A. A standardized, repeatable curriculum with weekly teaching outlines for both the teachers, and every class participant.

B. An initial New Member "starter literature packet" with key church-life literature and specially written inserts

C. Weekly introductions to key people in the church.

D. Video Victory reports, intros, humor and short segments of "New Member Video Catnip". Illustrate benefits of membership the best way: through edited, crisp 'benefit-testimonies' of former New Members now both Regular and Long-Term members.

E. A weekly chance for New Member Class participants to tell their "history", to tell their story, and to participate.

F. Acquire, in writing, previous church experiences and the "psychological contract" of New Member Class participants. "PSYCHOLOGICAL CONTRACT MEANS" their own personal expectations of the church, which must be acquired IN WRITING B-E-F-O-R-E they join. Every New Member has in his/her mind certain, specific expectations.

Identifying expectations before disappointing them, (even if unintentionally), is just smart. Since Information Equals Power, acquire this "psychological contract' early and avoid misunderstandings.

G. Clearly communicate (both in verbal and in written form) the church's own expectations. Too many churches only verbally communicate "their lowest level expectations to New Members (i.e. Sunday AM attendance, tithing), then later down the road they try to `lasso' NM's into small group or Sunday School attendance, involvement in personal ministry, etc.

2: Every New Member Literature Packet should include:

A) A welcome letter and literature. A nice warm welcome note or letter,perhaps even a copy of a handwritten letter from the pastor(s) is a nice personal touch. A photocopied handwritten letter is much more personal than the most precise typed or 600 D.P.I.laser printed form letter. Even the shortest handwritten note is even more impressive, and will probably be saved by the New Member among his/her valuables.

B. A pictorial directory of staff, leaders, preferably the latest church-wide pictorial directory as well of the entire church.

C. A printed copy of the church's philosophy of ministry statement, and of the church's missions statement. Also, if they exist, a copy of the church's 1, 2 and 5 year goals.

D. Explanation of denominational distinctives and practices is helpful.

E. A floor plan and map of the church facilities.

F. A New Member application should be included, one that contains adequate space (more then 3 lines) to describe how they came to a personal saving faith and relationship with the Lord Jesus.

G.   Finding out in writing what they liked and didn't like about the previous church(es) they used to be a part of is useful.

H.   How about a week by week sheet for T-H-E-M (NM's) to fill in throughout the New Member Class process, critiquing the highs and lows of each week's class, and suggestions for improvement.

Who knows more about the New Member orientation process and what it is like for the New Member to go through it? Right: the NM! As Peter Drucker puts it, "Over 75% of all new ideas already exist in the mind of the customers."

I.   A list of officers, deacons, leaders, and ministries, with a mini-description of each of the ministries listed.

#3. What part of Matthew Chapter 18 is crucial to the New Member Class?

In Matthew 18, verse 15, the Lord Jesus taught very specifically and powerfully on conflict resolution. He commanded: "If you have something against your brother, go talk to him alone." Isn't God's way of conflict resolution wonderful. Right there in the Bible, God spells it out, to prevent either overreacting in a non-healthy way, or just as bad, ignoring it, letting it grow infected, until it turns gangrenous, divisive, and causes some churches to split right down the middle.

Matthew 18:15-17 should be taught, prayed over, and discussed. Biblical, historical, and local church examples should be presented. New Members should covenant this into their hearts.

#4: The Ultimate "bonding" glue for New Members:

In Assimilating New Members, Lyle Schaller expertly teaches the best glue for New Members is to become part of a small group, (when possible), even before officially joining the church.Lyle

Schaller gives one example of this as those joining the choir and bonding to that groups members long BEFORE The New Member Day ever arrives.

More about bonding and small group dynamics under Back Door # 5: Regular Members in the next section.

#5: The #2 most powerful bonding glue for New Members:

The unbeatable bonding-power of small group involvement is followed by NM's finding a Role or Task to be regularly involved in as their ministry with the church. Involvement in ministry, (doing and giving, not just receiving), helps the church to become "**My**" church, not just "**the**" church or "**their**" church.

We'll also discuss this in more depth under Back Door #5. Helping New Members "bond" to a small group, and "find their ministry" is something that must be intentionally taken care of. It will not happen by osmosis, or default.

Sunday morning isn't the place to make friends. It is a launching place, but the waters of relationship there are far too swift and shallow to put the motor down into the water and "water ski."

#6: What might be a good ongoing component from each NM class?

Creating an ongoing small group out of each New Member class until the people in that group have all transferred out into other small groups in the church, is an idea worthy of consideration.

Giving a set 4 or 6 week ending point as well, will help its members settle down in another small group before the disbanding date.

#7: How can "overly-large" New Member classes be thinned out?

Fifteen to twenty New Members in a class is a maximum. Beyond that, each person is not going to be able to participate each week, or be heard.

One alternative is to hold New Member classes more frequently. Thus, you'll have fewer people "building up" in the "reservoir" ready for the next class. This facilitates giving more personalized treatment to the New Members in each individual class.

Greater frequency keeps the whole concept of New Member recruitment and development before the entire church, rather than making it an "obligatory" annual or twice a year function or event.

#8: What are some other New Member events done in churches?

Popular New Member events that many churches use include: Newcomers' nights, Newcomers' barbecues, Newcomers' small groups, off-site events, catered breakfasts or lunches, etc.

What New Member recruiting events do you use, or have you heard of? Please use the response coupon in back of this book to "seed" into my thought and share with me the best ideas you run across. Thanks.

Another important item, before New Member Reception service, is that New Member Sponsors should be in place. We will cover this after the next chapter, which will look at the Actual New Member Receiving Day and ceremony.

Chapter 28

New Member Receiving Day

1. Why should New Member reception service be held Sunday morning, not evening?

When possible, New Members reception service should be a Sunday Morning Worship service, rather than evening. This adds church-wide significance and more personal exposure of the New Member to the larger church family. Most churches draw 50% or less of their Sunday AM crowd to their PM service.

Whatever receives attention from the pulpit is what is perceived as important in the eyes of the believer in the pews. Thus, when New Member Reception is "main street, prime time" SUNDAY A.M. "FARE" (taking an entire Sunday AM service), it is endowed with much more importance. It becomes self-seeding for future NM classes, and NM reception days.

2. The larger the numbers in the New Member class being received, the more intentionalized the personalized treatment must be.

New Member receiving process in huge churches can become "cattle herding". The personalized treatment must be kept as a main ingredient and never "lost" in the shuffle. The megatrend is "High touch". A "low touch" quickie service will be remembered negatively and easily transform into a "let's go" touch. Preserving the "special-ness" of NM day can easily be bypassed.

3. New Member Reception Day Morning Service Could Include:

1. A video(or slide) extract "update" of former NM testimonies
2. A video (or slide show) of New Members being added.

3. Photo Poster-Boards (on easels in the lobby) featuring New Members, along with a small typed information paragraph about them and their families. We have all asked a new person their name at church once or twice, then again and again. We really wanted to get to know the person. But after asking fifty times or so, one finally gives up.

   Keeping the name, photo and information paragraph up a few months will greatly assist the entire church in bonding relationally, and assisting all in name-face recognition.

4. A New Member photo wallboard to stay up for the first 12 months. Having faces and names of (family members and name information easily accessible in the church lobby has priceless, beneficial effects.

   A) It makes the New Member feel the church values them, prioritizing learning their names, and helping them belong.

   B) It enables Church members to "refresh their memory", and then socially use that name until they learn it.

   C) It places the value of developing relationships before the entire church as a top priority. Separate wall boards could be in place for staff and their families, for departmental heads, Regular Members and LTM's (Long Term Members) we'll discuss later under Regular Member care.

4. Items to Include in the New Member Service:

A. Questions asked of each New Member should go beyond merely attending worship and tithing. Include unique testimony points, any role or task the specific NM may be committed to, as well as which Sunday School class (and/or care group)they will be a part of. Introduction of their sponsors along with each New Member is also crucial part of the service.

B.   The New Member induction sermon should also include and
      deal with the # 1 cause of New Member loss: unresolved
      conflict.Moravian churches used to include reading the
      passage out of Matthew 18: verse 15 which we've already
      discussed. Obtaining a verbal conflict resolution commit-
      ment from each prospective New Member is a powerful part
      of each New Member service.

C.   Since the #1 bonding glue for New Members is small group
      participation, and the #2 glue best glue involvement with a
      role or task, some churches strongly suggest, (while others
      require), all New Members join BOTH a care group and a
      church ministry B-E-F-O-R-E reception into membership.

D.   It is advantageous to have each New Member's Sponsor
      come upand be introduced right along with them in front of
      the entire congregation. This spreads the "sponsor concept"
      churchwide, helping recruit future sponsors. It also rein-
      forces the importance of intentionalized relationship build-
      ing throughout all areas of the church's life.

#5 Always include a New Member reception afterwards.

The reception is as important to New Member recognition as
it is after a wedding. In essence, the New Member is "marrying"
the church. This is the most important day in the relationship of the
New Member with your church. Refreshments and instrumental
music in the background should be included. What other touches
does your church add ?

6. After New Member Day items to include:

A)   Reprint NM photos and NM info in the next church bulletin.
B)   Start groups of NM's, until they "bond" into other groups.
C)   Implement an effective New Member Sponsor Program

Chapter 29

New Member Sponsorship Programs

No church wants to lose New Members. Yet, when asked what systems and programs are in place to prevent NM loss, answers are scarce. When New Members join your church, they're sincere in wanting to create a long-term committed relationship. **Since 50% of New Members drop out in the first year "at risk" period, churches need to "work smart" in New Member retention strategizing.**

The "New Member Sponsor" is not a new idea. It is found in the writings of the early church father Hippolytus (circa 215 A.D.). He wrote: "New Converts were given a three year apprenticeship, and an assigned S-P-O-N-S-O-R to guide converts into maturity, witness and service."

Winning the war against New Member loss is an attainable goal. In the secular arena, military weapons have improved over the centuries. A pastor once commented that one modern nuclear powered aircraft carriers with a fleet of F14's, & F16's, A4 Intruders, cruise and tomahawk missiles, etc could single-handedly have won World War II. Its superior weapons and radar technology could take out all the 1940's "state-of-the-art," (now obsoleted) weapons.

There was a time when no believer had the Bible in print. Even if they could get a copy, it was only in Latin. The average believer had no training in the cleric's "code" language . The printing press with moveable type invented by Johanne Gutenberg (1457) helped bring the Bible beyond the priests to the common man.

Martin Luther translated the Bible from the Latin Vulgate for the first time into the everyday language of the common man (German), equipping believers, and birthing the Reformation.

The entire concept of New Member Sponsors is a stealth "smart-weapon". This intentionalized assigning of a sponsor (a friend or paraclete) to every New Member for (and throughout) the critical first 12 months can help each New Member, to feel they're being helped to "belong", till they really do feel they belong.

#1   There are 2 main areas New Member's Sponsors Undergird:

1)   **Relationships** (the intentional development of)
2)   **Information**: to help make the church understandable to the New Member, explaining activities of both the church as a whole, and any individual's actions or program/church decision that might not be as clear.

#2   The New Member Sponsorship program must include:

A)   Written out, time-defined responsibilities.
B)   As part of the NM "entry path", the NM sponsor program must be highly intentionalized. It must have training, curriculum, recruitment, and a supervisor given oversight, authority, and accountability. It must be intentionalized.

#3.   Qualifications for New Member Sponsors must include:

A)   Not already overloaded (only having one other ministry).
B)   Faithful in prayer, and mature in modeling the Christian life.
C)   Faithful in reporting, and doing everyday "why do this" items

D) Length of service for a sponsor should be maximum one year.

E) Number of New Members a sponsor can sponsor is O-N-E.

#4: How can a Sponsor program fit into an already crowded churchministry program?

Some readers may be saying, all we need at our church is one more program. A good thing hospitals didn't react like that when cardiac care units were introduced? Sometimes new life-saving programs make other pre-existing programs "retire-able".

The measure of success in a Sunday school class (or any ministry) shouldn't be mere longevity. At Willow Creek, the measure is the changed lives it is currently producing for Jesus Christ.

#5: Other Miscellaneous New Member Sponsor Tips:

A) Hold annual New Member Sponsorship appreciation and recruiting dinners. This answers the question: "Where are we going to get these New Member sponsors from?"

B) On pages 45, 56, & 57 of Joel Heck's book, "New Member Application" is a New Member Sponsor recruiting bulletin insert, commitment forms, training tips, etc. Buy the book and don't "re-invent the wheel."

#6 The Two best resource books on New Member Sponsor Programs are:

A) "The First Year", by Suzanne Braden

B) "New Member Assimilation" by Joel Heck

Both can be ordered in our Resources Center Form at back of book.

Chapter 30

New Member Tele-Survey (and its application)

Remembering and implementing the megatrend concept of "High-Tech/Hi Touch" is vital to New Member care. A telecare "monitoring call" to all New Members (at the three month interval after joining) is a profitable strategy in helping NM's assimilate.

The concepts of tele-care,(and tele-prayer) are both compatible and very, powerful "bonding" ministries. However, using a telecomputer to auto-dial with a recorded message will defeat the intended purpose. The personal touch must be kept dominant.

The below survey is used from the must-read book, "Attracting New Members " by Robert Baste. This book is full of other world-class ideas for you to benefit from. The survey is adaptable for use in a Regular Member survey as well. The book is available thru our order form in back of this book.

How to use this New Member Telesurvey

Your church's current (or future) telecare team would call your New Members approximately 3 months after they've joined the church.

The purpose of the call is to listen to them and get both "hot and cold running information." If they're feeling good they'll be glad to share it. If they (New Members) are feeling badly, someone at the church needs to find out before negative feelings take them out Back Door # 6: Inactivity.

Following are 13 questions, and an introductory phone-team script for your telecare team to read, memorize, and improve on.

New Member Telecare survey: and sample opening script

"Hello, this is Ray VanGerwyn, calling on behalf of Pastor Scott Hagan and Harvest Church. Pastor is thrilled you and your wife recently joined Harvest Church as members. He asked us to call and help him by getting your feelings, and feedback, on a few questions to let us know how we're doing; help us do a better job.

Would this be a good time to get your answers to a few short questions, or would calling back at another time be better for you?

13 Suggested New Member Telecare Questions

#1 The first time you attended our church, what attracted you?

#2 What led you to make a return visit?

#3 Who did the most to make you feel at home?

#4 How long did you attend here before you decided to join?

#5 What made you want to join? Did anything make you hesitate?'

#6 Before coming here, were you ever active in another church?

#7. How did you first become aware of this church?

#8. How would you describe your experience during the New Member orientation process? How could it be improved ?

#9. Are there any church groups or activities you are currently taking part in (or might want to be a part of)?

#10. How did friends you've invited like our Sun AM service?

#11. What are your feelings about our worship services?

#12. Do you have any concerns about our church you wish to share?

#13. As a New Member, how has our church met your expectations?

You will notice: #12 and #13 are especially good "venting" questions, to generally enable the church(and its callers) to get at information that may be more "cold (or negative)."

Chapter 31

Questions To ask your New Members :

1) Sample your most recent NM crop using the Telesurvey.
2) Locate and survey NM's who did "drop out" since 50% usually do. If the social "code of silence" keeps you from getting that information, then send an survey mailing asking anonymous feedback with postage paid return-survey devices.
3) Survey New Members from the past 1,2,to 5 years who stayed with the church. Ask what challenges they faced, what helped them "bond" the most, and their ideas for improvement.

Questions to Ask of Your New Member Policies

1) Are our New Member policies written down?
2) Should our church develop a "New Member Care" Task Force to survey active and inactive NM's,and evaluate currently policy?
3) What is your current NM retention and dropout rate?
4) What NM policy improvements does your church need in the Immediate, Short, and Medium Term time range?

Chapter 32

Backdoor #5: Regular Members Intros

We now move on to winning the Back Door War in dealing with Back Door # 5: Regular Member losses. The code is RM's.

The Regular Member is the backbone and pillar of the church. He carries the load, pays the bills, fills the choir, does whatever needs to be done, signs on the mortgage for the new building extension, serves late hours on the board, seems to be the one who is "always there, every time the church doors are open."

Retaining Regular Members is absolutely and unarguably crucial. The next 20 plus pages will transmit specific tips, facts, and suggestions for improving RM care & retention.

#1: How many Regular Members are written off church roles yearly?

Data from the yearbook of American and Canadian churches reveals 2 - 3 million church members are written off church rolls yearly. Totally accurate numbers are probably multiplied times that, as churches are reluctant to "purge" their member rolls, reporting lower "numbers", feeding thoughts of decline.

#2: What fraction of Regular Members feel they just don't belong?

Between 1/3 and 1/2 of all church members surveyed said, "We don't really feel that we belong." Remember the two-circle (Membership and Fellowship circle) "Background Theory" we studied under New Members? It could be very beneficial to use it with RM's as well.

Find out where they're putting their "x" before their "non-belonging" pulls them further outward through Backdoor #6.

Pardon the pun, but how many think an "X-Ray" (background Theory check-up) is preferred, saving someone's life from cancer, rather than just letting them die.

#3: Can you identify and explain the 1:30 RM Care Growth Ratio below?

The 1:30 ratio (again from "Church Growth Ratio Book"), states that every RM ought to be contacted every thirty days by both a telecare/teleprayer team. A brief, sincere call stating "We just called to say we appreciate you in the church, and to ask if there's anything(or anyone) the prayer team can pray for in your behalf" can work wonders.

Regular Members are usually N-E-V-E-R CONTACTED BY THE church except when they are needed to DO something for the church. How do you feel about "friends" who only call when they NEED something from you, never just to see how you are doing? Some friends are drainers, others are replenishers. What kind of a friend to its RM's is your church?

RM's can feel overused and under-appreciated. They also can fail to be missed and feel whether they live or die, they're only appreciated for what they can do for the church, not who they are. When an RM feels that way, they're headed for Back Door #6.

#4 Which of the 16 Myths of Assimilation applies most to RM's?

The most deadly RM and NM myths are both the same: namely, that "J equals B". You know we're referring to myth: "Joining equals Belonging".

The truth is: "<u>Joining Does N - O - T Equal Belonging</u>"

A second deadly myth undermines RM care programs. It says: "When someone becomes a RM, nothing more remains to be done."

This leads to passive neglect. Regular Members can feel taken for granted. There's a story of farm couple in counseling. The man, when asked if he'd told his wife lately he loved her, replied: **"I told her I loved her when we married 30 years ago, and I'll be the first to let her know if (and when) anything changes."**

A similar story tells about another husband goes this way: **"I love my wife so much it's all I can do to keep from telling her!"**

People have to be told weekly, daily, regularly that they are loved and appreciated. Tell your husband or wife, kids, employees, church congregation and Regular Members, collectively and individually: they are loved, wanted, needed, and appreciated.

#5 Do Regular Members need as much high-touch as NC's, NM's & V's?

The answer is "Yes, Yes, and Yes! Yes they do. They need to be appreciated and loved." If you have Visitor appreciation dinners, and New Convert dinners, when are RM's appreciated and "dined"?

Regular Members pay the bills, staff the Sunday School and task forces, women's and men's ministry, the nursery, children's and youth ministry, etc. Often they can get to feel under-appreciated, especially in a growing church, where attention goes to the

Visitors, New Converts, and New Members.

In Luke 15's "Prodigal son" parable, who got all the attention? The returned prodigal receives the party (analogous to the V-1, 2, 3, NC and NM receptions). Meanwhile, the elder brother is like Regular Members who also need their emotional tanks kept full. The elder brother never went to the pigpen. Still, he developed an "internal pigpen"(an ingratitude-attitude) in his heart.

Where was all the attention being placed? On Back Doors #1, 2, 3, 4. Under-appreciated RM's can contact "elder-brother-itis". Sibling rivalry is another term for it. Prevention is the best cure for this preventable malady.

#6 Name 7 ways to stroke, encourage, "re-Bond" RM's ?

6.1 Create church lobby photo wall boards of RM, and LTM's. Give special honor to your **LTM's (Long TermMember's)**, just as on Mothers' Day churches honor the youngest and oldest moms. Listing the number of years a LTM has attended not only strokes "LTM"'s, but says to young Boomer families: "These people respect their elders and also respect longevity, loyalty and faithfulness. Nice touch!"

6.2 Update the church directory with a special LTM page in front.
Especially in an older, rapidly growing(and therefore more rapidly changing) church , a photo directory with a special LTM (Long Term Member) page in front, giving the length of years (25, 35, 50 years) membership gives a sense of honor, perspective, and stability to the entire church.

6.3 Give LTM's permanent name tags with length of years on them:
Different colored(silver, gold, white, red,) etc. permanent

name tags with the length of years as an Active Member is another way of appreciating RM's and LTM's. Perhaps a silver one for 25 years, a gold one for 40 or 50 years, etc.

6.4 Regular Member Appreciation Dinners:
Many churches have separate Newcomer, Visitor, and Sunday School worker appreciation dinners. Too few churches have regular appreciation banquets for their Regular and Long Term Members. No New Converts, New Members, or Newcomers are allowed at these events, except to testify and praise the RMs and LTM's. This is only for the RM core of your church. When a person's 'emotional tank' is full, they have no need to 'act out' to get attention. When a person can't get recognition for doing good, often they end up seeking attention in other ways.

#6.5 Short, concise "good-old"days video clips:
Interviewing RM's and LTM's for the highlights of their relationship with the church, can create powerful 1-2 minute clips. You could show it Sunday morning, or at select events, as well as weave bits of it into New Member class, New Convert class, Visitor Video catnip clips, etc.

#6.6 You could convene regular Member focus Groups
Focus Groups are groups you call together to get feedback on specific topics. Gathering RM and LTM focus groups on the subject of New Growth (particularly in a fast growing church), (so they feel listened to), can help them feel more comfortable with the "new people" flooding into a rapidly growing church.

Ask them for their ideas on how to blend the new growth with the older growth of the church. Let them know you're actively listening to their advice, and in no way going to forsake or forget them.

#6.7 <u>Use anonymous surveys to get and "vent" real feelings</u>

Enabling people to vent and really express how they feel is a vital dynamic in keeping RM's from "Back-door"ing. "Cold information" does not flow as easily as "hot information." Thus, anonymous surveys is another good element to add to RM care. A bulk-mailing survey to just those who are RMs and LTMs is one way to uncover unspoken feelings. Let them vent.

7: Five Ways to Interweave Regular Members and New Members are:

1. Have a Regular Member, and New Member of the week. Honor them with 60 (or even 30) seconds weekly from the pulpit. John Maxwell says: "Make heroes of your people."

2. Have an "RM and NM of the week" in each Sunday's bulletin. It could be the same person as from the pulpit, or could be two more people. Fill their emotional-tanks. Whatever receives attention from the pulpit is what is perceived as important.

3. Interweave New and Old Growth, by using both RM's and LTMs as New Member Sponsors. Feature them in NM Class Video clips also.

4. Have a proper balance of New Members, Regular Members, and Long Term Members on the church board. Don't allow a closed-off "good old boys" Board network where average board tenure is 20 or 30 years. If your church board merely re-shuffles every other year, what does that say to 'new growth', and New Members? It says : "Closed circle; no entry point."

Obviously, a New Convert shouldn't be put on the board, but if the Lord brings seasoned church board type people, they won't wait 25 years for the inner circle to become a possibility. Jack Hayford and Church on the Way allow only two terms on the board per lifetime.

When a Board accepts a New Member at the church for only two years (or less), it says to the new growth: "There's hope for new ideas, for new people like you, and for more new growth."

5. Involve New Members in selecting the Regular Member of the year, and of the week. If New Members are selecting and giving honor to Regular Members, the RM's pick up on that, as well as wanting the award or plaque, & recognition.

Chapter 33

Regular Members: Assimilation In and Thru Small Groups

Developing relationships is T-H-E supreme "glue" for bonding people to churches. Where does this best take place? **Relationships develop best in smaller group settings,** whether Sunday School groups, home care groups, or service task groups.

In the past 20 years, Sunday School nationally has dropped from 45 million to 28 million. Churches know this, but don't know why. Most of the following Small Group theory is applicable towards remedying Sunday School's national decline.

Most Sunday School teachers and supterintendents have never studied small-group theory. Most don't know the names Cho, Galloway, Lyman Coleman, Carl George, Ralph Neighbor, and others. They should!

Following is a summary of some of the best thoughts on Small Groups. It is less than the `tip of the iceberg' as to what is now available in many excellent resources dealing with this subject.

#1   Can you complete the phrase:
"_____ groups for _____ people"

"**New groups for New people**", means that new people will assimilate most efficiently and permanently into newer groups.

#2: By what age do small groups reach "saturation" and "closeout"?

Most groups reach saturation and encrustment before they are two years old. "Encrustment" means the hardening of the entry path. The group's social networks "establish" and it eventually becomes impossible for a newcomer to penetrate, bond and become part of that group. The newcomer will never be able to catch up to the group's "social history" as it gets older and older.

Carl George states that of all groups that don't multiply by the age of two, 90% never will. Any group not busy "birthing new life" will eventually close off to new life when it comes knocking.

#3: Name a few basic, small-group ratios and from the "Church Growth Ratio" book?

A. **1:5** 1 of every 5 groups should be less than two years old.Otherwise, too high a percentage of the groupshave already encrusted, which decreases a church's assimilation which cuts off growth. A church plateaus when its smallgroups are at saturation.
B. **75:100** 75 of every 100 Regular Members should be involved in a small group.
C. **90:100** A healthy expectation for New Members is that 90%of them should (and will) get involved in a group.

#4: How do inclusiveness and exclusiveness factors grow and operate in a group as it ages?

This, once again, is borrowed from Lyle Schallers classic text on Assimilation: "Assimilating New Members".

<u>In a New Group: High inclusion but low Fellowship Factor</u>

In a new group, inclusiveness is high. If somebody's starting a new class with 2 or 3 people, when a new couple comes, doesn't it make sense the new class "jumps on" the newcomers with hospitality and an invitation to a meal out afterwards, etc.? Desire to include newcomers is high, because the group is little and totally new. To a new group of four, adding two people represents a 50% growth in one Sunday. Inclusion is high, but fellowship (the group history) is low.

<u>In an Older Group. High fellowship, Lower Inclusion</u>

In older groups the dynamics reverse. Fellowship (the group's social history) is high, but inclusion of new people is low. Everybody's got their relationships already carved out. The newcomer can never catch up with the past events.

#5: Name the Top Seven Classic Small Group Mistakes to avoid:

<u>Mistake # l: Geographic Assignment:</u>

Mandating that people who live in a certain area must attend certain small groups is a classic mistake. Cho, Galloway, Carl George, Jim Dethmer, Bob Logan are all agreed on this point.

People can be invited to, informed of, and referred to the geographically nearest group to where they live. They will end up where they have friends or the highest affinity/shared interest.

People like to be among their own kind, and would rather drive across town to an "affinity-match" group than drive two blocks to be with people they have nothing, (or very little), in common with.

<u>Mistake # 2:   Letting groups teach what they please</u>

Cho found this out by first-hand experience. He describes the mini-church split in his excellent book, "Successful Home Cell Groups". Now with almost 70,000 small groups active at his church in Seoul, he's an small-group authority you might consider heeding.

The weekly small group theme or lesson can be an extension of your Sunday sermon theme, or be tied into current Sunday School curriculum, an approved course book from Serendipity, NavPress or Christian Twelve-step Recovery-Support sources. The point is that the teaching must be pre-approved, assigned and designed.

Cho, Willow Creek, and many others now provide one year small group outlines and lessons to customize, and use.

Mistake #3: Letting groups meet without reporting back:

This is a classic warning signal, according to Small Group expert, Pastor Dale Galloway, whose church, New Hope Community Church in Portland, Oregon, runs 5,000 with 95% active in 500 small groups.

Mandatory weekly report-back must be stressed in Group Leader Training class and curriculum. It must be expected and inspected. People don't always do the expected; they tend to do the inspected.

"If the leader of a care group is UNFAITHFUL in reporting back, and after adequate intervention continues that way, he is not qualified to lead a registered, church-sanctioned group. If necessary, a non-reporting group leader is asked to step down. According to Galloway: "he's going to become a loose cannon,and you (the unity and vision of the church) will become the target."

Mistake #4: Not having specific growth goals for the group.

This is a common mistake in both home groups and most Sunday Schools. Over 95% of most Sunday Schools, if asked, "Do you have specific numerical growth goals,"would answer : "No".

This is equivalent to playing basketball on a court with a ball, a backboard, two teams,etc. but no rims on the backboards to give closure when a goal is actually made. Both teams would 'claim' to have shots 'go in' but who would be the judge. Many Sunday Schools are "playing basketball without a hoop".

At Cho's church, every group targets the adding of one new unchurched person every 6 months to their group. Semi-annual progress is reported, and group leaders are held accountable. Cho explains that he gathers the leaders of those groups who failed to add the new person in the prior six months. He tells them "God is not pleased with you. You are not being like the profitable servant in Matthew 25 that multiplied His Master's talents. God wants to say "well done, good and faithful to you." To help you, you must be disciplined, and go for a whole night of prayer and fasting to Prayer Mountain."

Prayer Mountain (Cho's church's prayer center) is 50 miles from Seoul, with a facility seating 10,000 people filled every Friday night to overflowing. The church's prayer warriors come to worship, pray and praise. Even when full, this is a smaller crowd to Cho. There are also scores of individual "prayer caves" where people may isolate themselves for renewal, and revival.

The reality of Yoiddo Full Gospel Church, where Cho pastors, is that the church is built on prayer, not small groups.

Mistake #5: Letting 'Koinonitis,' become lethal & contagious:

'Koinonia' is the Greek word for fellowship. Peter Wagner coined the phrase "Koinonitis" to denote the deadly dynamic taking place both in Small Groups,and Sunday School classes that become ingrown. Koinonitis" occurs when a group "falls in love with itself". Sunday School classes, once evangelistic and effective in both reaching the lost and assimilating new people, can become "donut chewing, spiritual navel-gazing" examples of `fellowship inflammation or 'Koinonitis'. There is a cure, and prevention.

Eventually a group becomes "self-focused", closed and encrusted, unless it is intentionally, continually re-targets for growth and multiplication into new groups and classes.

Growth goals, and using the "E" seat"(or empty evangelism seat that is prayed for each week) always provides at least one empty chair representing the person God may bring to the group next week by some group member inviting them.

Mistake #6: No Apprentice and Leadership development in place

Healthy small groups are the perfect place for apprenticing and developing leadership for new groups. When this is done as the norm, there are always new leaders ready when new groups need to be birthed.

Carl George's masterpiece, "Prepare Your Church For The Future" (published by Fleming Revell, 1990) explains this in depth.

Mistake #7: Allowing small groups to grow too large.

When healthy growing groups realize the expected "norm" is that they reproduce into a new groups, the excitement and adventure of producing new life overshadows the sadness of seeing the group's members voluntarily "ship out" to help nucleate new groups.

A group ceases to be a small group above 12-14 members. Beyond that point, everyone can't participate and be heard, be cared for, and be adequately missed; it has ceased to be a "small group". When all don't participate because of size, the people who usually get "left out" are those needing care, and participation the most.

6: How can church-wide plateau from small groups being at saturation point be pro-actively prevented?

Continually enabling and expecting groups to grow and multiply is both the prevention of (and cure for) "Plateau and Decline" disease. Any Sunday School class not intended for growth ,by default, will become a breeding place for `Plateau-itis' or "flat-line disease".

7 What basic laws of Small Group theory are many non-growing Sunday School classes breaking?

The "Top 7 Small Group mistakes" listed above are operative in most non-growing Sunday School classes. These mistakes include: size, age over two years, absence of specific numerical growth goals, absence of the "E" chair", a lack of intentionalized apprentice development, a lack of intentionalized, multiplication of new groups, and the lack of continually starting new groups.

8 Can you intelligently discuss "Meta-theory" and "Jethro II" from the book "Prepare your Church for the Future", by Carl George.

Put this book at the top of your "must read" list. After your Bible, make this book the other #1 priority reading daily until you get it read. It will provide massive, positive, impact on your life and ministry.

This is the best book about ensuring the "span of care", raising up leadership, apprenticing new leaders, and successfully implementing Small Group ministry in churches that have failed at it several times before, as many unfortunately have.

This book is a synthesis of the 'best' in small-group theory. The concept(and benefits) of a church-wide monthly "Leadership Community", is worth the price of the book. Buy it. You'll love it!

Chapter 34

Regular Members: Assimilation through Roles and Tasks (R&T)

Developing healthy relationships is done chiefly through the small groups, and secondarily, through member involvement in a role or task. Below are some pointers on this vital area, as it relates to winning the Back Door war in retaining, and developing RM's.

#1: Explain the below "Role & Tasks" member-mobilization ratios. (Once again, from the 'must read' "Church Growth Ratio Book")

A: 60:100   40:100,   and 20:100

A healthy, growing church should have 60 roles or task opportunities for every 100 Sunday morning attenders. These do not have to be separate tasks, but are combined involvement opportunities in tasks available. 15 Ushering opportunities would count for 15 of the 60 opportunities a church of 100 should have. It could be 5 letter writers, 6 bakers, 25 choir members, rest home visitation teams, offering counters, etc.

Since Role and Task involvement is a close second from the very top as far as gluing people into a church, the less Role or Task opportunities, the lower the assimilation will be.

Plateaued churches usually have 40 roles or tasks per 100, while declining churches have 20 or less roles per 100 attenders.

These quantifiable vital signs can help focus the Member Mobilization "big picture" and can lead to practical diagnosis.

#2 Review a few volunteer "new realities" vs. "old realities:" and the ways they affect all churches today

2.1 <u>**Time: As George Barna puts it, "Time is the new currency".**</u>

The phrase "Time is Money" is age-old. But the application of it, to management of church volunteer work, is exponentially different in the Information Age setting.

People in the 1990's have the same 168 hour week and 1440 minute day they've always had. Yet they increasingly "have less and less time."

With 60% of moms and dads working outside the home, the double—working profile will rise to 80-85% by the end of the '90's. Churches will increasingly run into the mobilization barrier, more and more people saying: "I'D LIKE TO HELP, I JUST DON'T HAVE TIME".

To catch volunteer co-ministers in the 90's, one is going to again have to "think like the fish they're trying to catch."

2.2 <u>**Radio Station K- WIIFM:**</u>

The average churchgoer today comes in with the code imprint of the "Me" generation all over him. He doesn't show up, stating, "Here I am pastor, what can I do to help". The majority today show up tuned in to station K-WIIFM ("What's In It For Me") saying: "Here I am, these are my felt needs; what can this church do for me?"

2.3 <u>**The "V Word" versus the "P word" or "M" word:**</u>

The word Volunteer (otherwise known as the "V word"), in past generations simply meant an unpaid chance to help a worthy cause. Increasingly, to the "Me" Boomer generation, the word Volunteer, though, is N—O—T a "User-Friendly word".

The word `Volunteer' increasingly translates as "flunkey" or V ictim slated for certain, future burnout, at a task one is usually neither qualified, nor gifted by God for, for which one will receive no training, and only be called in to `put out the fire' as an extension of a current "crisis management" operation." The negative connotations of the word far outweigh its positive ones to the majority of Boomers today.

Far more attractive, and productive, is the use of words like: Partners in Ministry, Volunteer Ministry network, Co-ministers, or Lay Ministers if you must use the unscriptural "L Word". Why not just call them what God calls them: ministers of the Gospel?

The priesthood of the believer was restored vertically in 1517 by Martin Luther, but the horizontal day-by-day ministry of every believer is still a reformation away. Too many clergy fear losing their power or position by "giving the ministry to their people". Meanwhile, it is the very thing that causes them eventually to lose the very "church" and ministry they're holding onto so tightly.

The priority needs for Boomers today are not survival, food or shelter. Rather, the top needs are for "meaning in Life", (level 4 and 5 on Maslowe's Hierarchy of Need) and a divine purpose or destiny.

The ministry of every believer is scripturally central to the fulfillment of the Great Commission. It's absolutely vital, and built right into God's original design and plan. God's Divine plan for mobilizing A-L-L of His children in ministry tragically takes a deadly backseat ride to "traditional programming".

God calls all His people to be "co-laborers with Him" (I Cor. 3:9). In Ex.19:6 God pronounced Israel a "Kingdom of priests"

4:   The Parable of the 1 million Pennies:

People don't have the time they used to have. Mom and dad are out of the house. Moms at home used to make up the largest share of church volunteer labor. They are no longer available.

All this notwithstanding, Boomers will take over the church before 2000 AD, according to Elmer Towns. All these Boomers, with so little time, ruling the church? Scary thought to some.

Let me ask: which would you rather have, ten $100 bills which total $1000, or a pickup truck-load of 1 million pennies($10,000)?

Which would you rather have? The bills or the pennies? I ask that in a room full of ministers, most raise their hand for the ten $100. Every time its the same "old, 'easy' thinking".

When I ask people "If you accept the pennies, what have you got?" Instead of saying "ten times more money"(or profit), once the response was: "With the pennies, you get a whole lot more work."

I respond to that, "yes . . . and no". "You get ten times more money, $10,000 instead of $1000, and yes, you DO get the potential of more work, UNLESS you commit to work smarter, not just harder."

Looking at 1 million pennies, managerially, isn't such a heinous task at all. It can be a quite enjoyable way to earn $9000 or $10,000. You just have to look through a different lens. A managerial lens gets the work done through other people, rather than doing all the work oneself. In a word: it's DELEGA-TION.

Now back to the one million pennies.

What if I choose to call our church Youth Pastor and say: "Craig, I've got a million pennies that need to be rolled into $1 penny rolls of 100 each. Tell me: are you interested in earning $500 for yourself this Saturday, another $250 for your kids to divide among themselves at $6 an hour, as well as $250 for your next youth ski trip or favorite missions project? What do ya say?"

Now you know as well as I do, any youth pastor that can honestly earn $500 in one Saturday has already said yes!

Did I end up with a whole lot more work, or a whole lot more money? I end up $9000 ahead <u>without any extra work at all</u>, other than re-thinking the process, "working smarter not harder".

Application: the Parable of the
1's, 2's, 5's, 10's and 20's.

Think of the hundred dollars and the pennies as units not just of money, but of time, since "time is the new currency".

The pre-Boomer volunteer work force used to donate 5, 10, and 20 hours per month. **They are the "5's, 10's and 20's".** They are a thing of the past.

The pennies? These are the people of the Ninety's. Time is the scarcest commodity they have. A recent survey revealed they feel they have 31% LESS free or leisure time than they had only 5 years ago.

They are not going to donate 5, 10 or 20 hours a month. They W-I-L-L donate one or two hours a month, or quarter. These are the "1's and 2's"(the new volunteer work force). They can make you "rich" if you look at them through the proper, managerial and generational lenses.

The one million pennies and the hundred dollar bills? They are those of the preceding, Pre-Boomer generation. Those who chose the ten $100 bills made the wrong choice. The smarter ones chose the one million pennies. They didn't choose more work, they just chose to work smarter, and delegate the work to more players. They came out nine or ten times ahead of those with "old thinking".

Now the Application:

Choosing the pennies in Volunteer ministry rather than the now non-existent "5's, 10's and 20's" is how growing churches are growing. There are no $100 bills any more, but there is an oversupply of under-appreciated, under-managed "1's and 2's".

Churches have for too long over-relied on, (and abused), the "5's, 10's and 20's", burning out their "super-committed, super-star" volunteers. In most churches volunteers are asked to commit to a life-sentence, or at least: "will you serve monthly,(which might be a 5) or weekly (more like a "10 or a 20")

My question: can you find and "cash in"(for Kingdom of God advantage) more 5's, 10's and 20's or "1's & 2's" ? Re-read this chapter if you are still in doubt.

Under-involvement of most members: #1 church problem in America.

The #1 church problem is getting more people involved in ministry of any type. At one end, there are too few people with too much work to do. At the other end of the spectrum, are the majority of God's people who have no regular ministry involvement at all.

Is there a way to equalize the two ends of the spectrum? Only by working "smarter", not harder. Churches must rethink member ministry mobilization.

Couldn't churches use volunteers less than weekly or monthly? Some might say here, "If people can't serve weekly or monthly, they're not worth the trouble, they 'ain't spit' in God's eyes."

Hold on just a minute! If someone offers the devil an hour or two a year, will he take it? You know he will. Now ,if someone offers God an hour or two a year, will He take it. Trick question! Go slow! In Luke 23, a thief on a cross was moments from death, but he offered God the final few minutes of his life, and did God take them! Hello!

Is there a way churches could offer volunteer ministry to individuals on a less than weekly or monthly basis? Yes, but only if we're willing to rethink our ministry involvement grids, and drop prejudices against 1's and 2's. **"Remember the pennies!"**

Working off a quarterly grid instead of monthly or weekly.

Instead of thinking weekly and monthly, church and ministry leaders need to rethink their recruitment grid. Remember how we learned to find the lowest common denominator back in elementary math. Think beyond 1 out of 1 (weekly) or one out of four(monthly). How about every 6 weeks, every 8 weeks, or even every 12 weeks?

So called 'normal' weekly/monthly work-slots must be re-configured to create more work opportunities of smaller proportion, and less frequency. Incremental entry level ministry opportunities are the order of the day (and the Age).

Remember the million pennies. Who came out ahead ?

Why not begin using quarterly sign up grids. That way, a person can sign up for any portion of a twelve week grid, at 6 week intervals, 10 week intervals as well as weekly or monthly for those with the time (the few remaining, 5's, 10's and 20's).

When a person volunteers (or is even recruited for member-ministry), inform them they can sign up for as little as once a quarter (or every 12 week), (even once a year) and that whenever they can help, it will be appreciated.

The vital thing is to get them involved in some form of ministry. Then, and only then, they can graduate from being a "1, to becoming a "2 , 3 or 4 ".

The computer and Binary Code: The Information Age:powered by mere, puny 'Zeros and ones'

Part of the genius of the computer is that its power is based on binary code. Binary code, is basically two rows of horizontal boxes (on top of each other) numbered from one to nine. Each of these is either in an on or an off position. The 1's represent the 'on position', the '0's the off position. These on and off combinations are the tiny units that give the millions of "calculations-per-second" capability to the computer.

Thus every number and letter in a computer (despite handling millions of computations per second),is all based on 9 boxes, with each box representing a series of combinations of 1's and O's, which in turn power individual switches into on or an off position.

The 1's used in binary code stands for the on position, the `0', stands for the off position.

Let's relate this to volunteer ministry. The hardest part of pushing a stalled car, is breaking inertia: getting it rolling.

Relate this to mobilizing stalled members into ministry at your church. What position are most church members in: the off or the on position. "The off" position? Correct Answer! To what position do you want them moved to? The "On position".

If they can be brought to A-N-Y active involvement at all, the Holy Spirit, (and NOT condemnation), can lift them to their maximal level of service. Remember why the Master only gave 5,2,and 1 talents in Matthew 25? Scripture tells us:"according to their ability".

Are more people going to move to an "on" position by asking them to be a 5,10, 20, or by accepting their 1 or 2 hours per quarter (or twice quarterly) ability and capability of helping?

There's more to this subject in a book I am working on, which I'm tentatively titling "100 Smart Ideas for Smart Pastors and Smart Churches".

Applying the million pennies analogy to entry-level ministry opportunities, (by re-thinking and decreasing the frequency of time-commitment asked of uninvolved people) can increase Kingdom production by a 9 or 10 factor at your church.

"Informationites"(Information Age people) expect church leadership to realize "1's and 2's" (one and two hour segments) are all the time many can give. Smart churches recognize this, ending up ahead 9 - 10 times of those waiting for the non-existent "5's, 10's and 20's" of yesteryear.

#4: Best ways of recruiting versus most common ways:

Recruiting people is usually done the reverse of the best way it can be done. In other words, the most commonly used methods are: 1) the pulpit, 2) the church bulletin, 3) letters, 4) telephone 5) asking the person face to face .

Research in churches has proven that the exact reverse of these most common methods is the most effective.

Most effective is: #1)   Asking the individual in person.

2nd most effective: #2)   A personal telephone call

3rd most effective: #3) Using letters

4th most effective: #4) Using the bulletin

5th most effective: #5) The pulpit

#5: Name a few good and bad motivations, and "down-line" payoffs

A) Bad motivations include:
1. **Guilt:** "I'll feel bad if I don't do it."
2. **Pride:** "I can do it better than anyone else", or "After I do it, I can tell everyone I did. "
3. **Resignation:** "Someone needs to. It might as well be me."
4. **Obligation:** "I don't want to, but I know I ought to, so..."

B) Good motivations include:
1. **Gratitude to God:** "Lord, this is my small way to thank You."
2. **Act of worship:** "Lord, I praise You as I'm doing this."
3. **"Love overflow":** "Lord, I love You and that's why I do it."

#6 Describe benefits of Willow Creek's Gift-Based Member-Ministry Mobilization-Network Program

Perhaps the best member-mobilization program in the USA is Willow Creek's "Network" (Member Ministry Placement Program). The overview video cost is $25, the benefits are priceless. In brief, it is a four week Member Mobilization course that teaches on:

1) A Biblical basis and philosophy of Ministry for every believer,
2) A Biblical basis for spiritual giftings,
3) God's plan and purpose of spiritually gifting every believer,
4) Several spiritual Gift Identification tests and instruments,
5) A brilliant workbook with 154 ministry job descriptions,
6) **The concept of Spiritual Gift placement advisors, and advice on "placement interviews",** follow-through and follow-up.

It is between Steps 4 and 6 that ministry placement in most churches stalls. Most churches teach spiritual gifts, and hold Spiritual Gift Identification workshops.

Too commonly, though, they leave out the identifying, "job-descriptions" for their church ministries, as well as having no Ministry Placement advisors, and no Placement interviews.

"Network" brilliantly, simply, and systematically provides all of the above, plus much more than I can describe here. Too many churches have a fatal "we've got to create it all ourselves" mental-block which keeps them from completing the very program that "Network" provides them "ready-made".

"Network" is designed to run on 4 consecutive Wednesday nights(with weekly homework assignments). It can be A) crunched into a one day weekday format, B) utilized in quarterly Sunday School format, or used however you deem best at your church.

"Network" components available (for less than $100 total)

include a 45 Minute Video overview of the whole "Network" program, a Leader's guide with answers, the participant's workbook, Leader's tape series(8 pack) and 12-pack recording of the whole seminar as taught by the originator, Bruce Bugbee. He is still head of Network at Willow Creek.

#7 Placing "the triangle gift" people in "triangle" ministries

Your church can escape the stereotypical dysfunction of having "non people-persons" greeting at the door, etc. A head usher once told me: **"We're trying to teach our greeters how to say hello to people"**.

The "norm" is mobilizing people by need, rather than identifying giftings of our people, and then identifying the ministries that utilize these giftings. Finally, through ministry placement advisors, you can logically link up people with the "mercy gift" into "mercy-gift based" ministries.

Chapter 35

Questions for Your Regular Members and RM Policies

What questions need to be asked now that we've covered RM's? Have you been asking the right questions? Here's a few more to consider:

Questions to Ask Your Regular Members:

1) What % of your church's RM's feel they don't belong? Why?
2. What can be done to help them feel more like they belong?
3) What questions in a congregational self-study would help?
4) What would your RM's like to see in additional programs?
5) What type of new small groups would draw those not in one?
6) Is it easy or hard for an RM to find ministry involvement less frequently than once a month?

Questions to Ask Your Regular Member Policies:

1) What are your current Regular Member losses?
2) What have R.M.losses been over the past 2,3,4,and 5 years?
3) Are these losses acceptable? Identify causes and cures .
4) Is a 'Regular-Member Care' Task Force a current need ?
5) Can your RM's vent "Cold Information" before they go Inactive? Anonymously? How? and How often?
6) Would bringing in a growth consultant help to identify, problems, solutions on RM losses?

Questions for Your Small Group Policies

1) What percentage of your small groups are over 2 years old?
2) Has "small group" theory been taught to your Sunday School teachers?
3) Are your member-ministry involvement ratios 60:100?

Chapter 36

Back Door # 6: Inactives:
(Code " I.A.'s")

Winning the Back Door War in closing Back Door # 6: Inactives (both in prevention and recovery) is a never ending battle; IA's (our code for Inactives) exist at every church.

Even as this chapter is read, people are incrementally going Inactive at every church world-wide. The question is: who is going Inactive, and why? What are healthy percentages of Inactivity? And what are the best prevention and recovery techniques?

When marriage breakdowns result in a separation, the stated #1 cause is a lack of communication. People go (and stay) Inactive due to this cause more than any other. If communication is not restored, separations deteriorate into divorce, just as Back Door #6 (Inactivity) deteriorates into Back Door #7, producing "Dropouts": and permanent loss.

#1: How does a church's definition of Active Member relate to the Inactivity level ?

How a church defines Inactive has a direct correlation to how that church defines active or healthy member?

How does your church define active members?

A)   Attends worship three times a month minimum? (two?)
B)   Also attends a small group/Sunday school? (how frequently?)
C)   Is regularly active in a Role or Task Ministry?
D)   Gives regularly to the church?

Whatever your definition of Active, Inactive must then be defined as the inverse of your definition. **A-L-L churches need, but too few have, a definition of Active or Inactive.**

What lack of attendance, or number of absences in a month, signifies Inactive at your church? At what number of Sunday absences is someone considered Inactive? . . . when they miss church two, three, four Sundays in a row, or when?

<u>The church's expectations influence Inactive levels:</u>

Another direct influencer on Inactivity is the 'degree of expectation' a church has of its members. Expectations set too high produce a high degree of burnouts, and a higher number of people going Inactive from that excess. Conversely, setting expectations too low will also create a high level of Inactives.

#2 Compare business customer-relations and IA prevention/recovery?

Jesus said in Luke 16:8 "The children of this world are wiser in their generation than the children of light." He was saying worldlings take care of business more astutely than Kingdom people. Successful business people know that "customer service" and public relations are "life and death" for their business.

The customer is the only one bringing money in the door of a business. In reality, the business is there for the customer. The multiplier factor for keeping a repeat customer versus generating a new customer is verifiable at 11: 1, or more.

Nordstrom is world famous for its customer service. An article was written called "The Gospel According To Nordstrom". They reward and prime their sales people to go the extra mile, (two or three) to keep their customers satisfied.

John Maxwell refers to the "1:11:55 principle": that one dissatisfied customer will go out and tell 11 others, who in turn will tell five others, so 55 people receive negative messages.

#3   Can you define and utilize the "6-8 week window" to advantage?

The "6-8 week window" is an identified disengagement and testing period in which the Inactive gives the church "6-8 weeks" to notice they're missing, and to respond appropriately. This includes identifying "the why" (or reason) the Inactive has gone IA. The Inactive is saying: "Do you want me, do you miss me?"

The IA is putting his relationship with the church on the line because for whatever reason, he/she is not satisfied with the relationship. Beneath the surface lies their unresolved conflicts.

At some point along this "6-8 week window," the IA says to himself, "I'm not really missed, since no one has contacted me." They reason: "I could have died, and no one would have noticed it, except perhaps in the newspaper obituaries." This makes them question their church relationships all the more.

If Inactivity goes beyond the "6-8 week window", (and no one contacts him/her), they will go from Inactive to Dropout. What is your church's care-delivery and safety-net in this time frame. Unless that lack of communication, and conflict gets resolved, separation turns to divorce, and the Inactive will Drop-out.

#3   What three things must a church know (and do) both before (and immediately after) a RM goes Inactive?

3.1 A church must have the information incoming, so that the Inactive (in process) is missed right away.

3.2 A church needs an effective system already operative so it can"kick into gear" immediately.

3.3 A church needs to put that system into action as soon as possible with all that go Inactive.

#4 Explain the concept (and coding) of A-l's, A-2's, and A-3's.

At Harvest Church, we have a system in place that activates specific ministry whenever anyone misses one week, two, and three weeks in a row.

We give absentees code names according to their absences: An A-l is someone missing one week, an A-2 misses two weeks, and an A-3 is someone missing three weeks in a row.

An "A-l" receives a postcard handsigned from the church stating they were missed by their family at Harvest that Sunday.

An A-2 (absent two weeks in a row) gets a phone call from a care team.

An A-3, (absent 3 times), triggers an automatic call from the Senior Pastor (or Staff) so that they are being personally contacted before they get more than halfway out the "6-8 week window".

#5: What are 5 standard warning signs of soon-to-be Inactives:

A) A change in attendance patterns at regular worship events.

B) A change in seating patterns (sitting farther back)

C) Lack of involvement in their regular Role or Task

D) Change of pronoun describing 'their' to 'your' church

E) A change in regularity of their financial giving

#6: 7 reasons Regular Members go Inactive:

A) Broken relationships

B) Unmet expectations

C) Tragedy or crisis

D) Unhealed hurts

E) Unrequited love: feeling their love for the church is "1-way"

F) They "graduate": meaning because of a legitimate special need,whether the skill-level of concert choir, or a special class for a special needs child, they transfer elsewhere

G) Reversion, or spiritual backsliding.

#7: 6 ways to increase church leader and member communications are:

7.1 Suggestion Box : This is a powerful communication tool.
Publicly encouraging church members to hand in ideas, (and "hot and cold information"), acts like vitamins taken regularly to prevent bodily health breakdowns and "Inactive-itis."

7.2 Listening-Line
Increasing numbers of businesses are opening 1-800 customer listening lines. A local church with a listening line doesn't need an 800 number, but can position itself favorably in the community (among Pre-Visitors all the way through to Regular Members and Inactives) as "the church that is listening to you" or simply, **"The church that is listening!"**

7.3 Victory reporting system: Intentionally gathering victory reports from the congregation is an Information-Age" smart-weapon few churches utilize. It could be on its own separate form in the pew rack, or detachable as part of the bulletin, or on the back of registration or prayer cards. It is also good for weekly, monthly and a cumulative year-long Victory-report publications.

7.4 Question of the week: Previously covered under Pre-Visitors.

7.5 Letter of the week: Communication between church members and leadership through letters is another "zero-cost" communication channel. Pulpit use of "permission-granted" excerpts can bless and unify the entire church.

7.6 Inactive Recovery Task Force: This is a vital ministry for churches that have their other Back Doors covered well first. The next chapter will given foundational information for such a Task Force.

Chapter 37

Lyle Schaller's 14 Assumptions About Inactives:

Lyle Schaller, in his classic textbook Assimilating New Members, has an excellent chapter on Inactives. Below is a sample of the entire book's brilliance, which is "must" reading for anyone serious about winning the Back Door War.

Schaller gives these 14 Assumptions re: Ministry to Inactives:

1. Assume all who joined the church as members did so in sincerity. They didn't join your church to deceive anyone. They really wanted to belong. They still do.

2. Assume each Inactive has in his mind a good reason for going Inactive. In their minds, they're justified in doing what they're doing.

3. Until that reason is identified and eliminated, the Inactive is going to stay Inactive.

4. To guess the reason for going Inactive is less productive than to discover it by talking to the Inactive and getting some communication flowing.

5. Inactives will initially offer excuses, not the real reason for disengaging from the church. The "code of silence" will at first keep "root reasons" from surfacing.

6. We will learn more by active listening than by talking. Expect to spend at least several hours.

7. It will likely take 6-7 hours(not just 2-3 hours) to uncover the root causes. Its not going to happen in one visit.

8. It will probably require not one, but several visits.
9. The longer we wait after someone goes Inactive, the more difficult reactivation is going to be. Most churches have never heard of the concept of an ongoing IA Reactivation Team.
10. Assume that no pre-existing class or group can specialize in-depth. You can't just hand this ministry off to an existingSunday School class, and say "why don't you guys do Inactive recovery. ("That's like picking a phone booth and saying "let's open a brain surgery center.") It is a specialized process, and it's will require special people, given special training.
11. Since Inactives already feel negative emotions, only specially chosen individuals should be trained and sent on Inactive recovery missions. You certainly don't want to send people that will make them feel worse.
12. Inactives send a warning signal which is called the "6-8 week window". During this time, they test the "caring and "will they miss me" reaction of the church (or lack of one)
13. Some RM's "graduate" (as Lyle Schaller puts it) either through experiencing new needs, or needing/desiring higher skill training, talent-pool level challenges, etc. This is not a negative type of Inactivity.
14. When ministering to Inactives, we must really listen, and challenge the assumptions that we all bring with us.

Chapter 38

Questions to ask your Inactives & Inactive Policies

Questions for Your Inactives:

1) What events led you into becoming Inactive?
2) What kind of things could we as a church do to keep other people from going Inactive?
3) How long did it take us to notice that you had gone Inactive?
4) Should we react to consecutive absences as we do, or how can we improve the caring ("missing") quotient of our church?
5) What can we do to make you feel part of our church again?
6) If its too late for #5 above, at what point did it become too late and why?(in your own words, feelings and thoughts?)

Questions for Your Inactive (I.A.) Policies:

1) How many are currently Inactive at our church, or going IA?
2) Track our church's IA's in the last 1, 2 & 5 years?
3) Do we have specific policies as to automatic ministry when someone is an A-l, A-2, or A-3 ?
4) Does our church have a concrete, written definition of what an Active Member is, and what an Inactive member is?
5) Are we (as a church and leadership) aware of the "6-8 week window" dynamic, and utilizing it to maximal advantage?
6) Do we need to create an ongoing Inactive Recovery Task Force?
7) Do we have the essential information regularly incoming (and being processed) so we contact IA's before they are too far gone?

Chapter 39

Back Door # 7: Dropouts Code ("D.O.")'s)

To a certain extent, things true about Inactives are also true about Dropouts. Therefore some material here will not only seem, (but actually be), redundant. Similarities though, are heightened and "relationships gone wrong" are in a more advanced state.

The "separation" in the marriage analogy has now turned into a divorce; the bad cold has turned into bronchial pneumonia, the infection has worsened into gangrene.

Let's take a closer look at the Inactive/Dropout continuum process, and some ideas in Winning the Back Door War against "Dropsy".

#1: The two main groups of Dropouts are:

Group A)   Those who drop out from your church, and

Group B)   Those who drop out from church in general; these folk say: "I'm burned-out on church, or I'm finished with church in general."

#2 Why do dropouts dropout?
Can you name the top six reasons?

1)   Unresolved conflict,
2)   Unmet expectations
3)   Burnout. Leadership needs to show its care and concern for workers by preventing burnout BEFORE it occurs. A pastor had his church grow from 40 to 150 in a year. A certain care group leader was slowly "burning out."

I advised: "better close the care group than lose that leader."

The pastor went to his group leader and said: "it looks like you're having some challenges at home, working a double job, etc. The group is probably too much of a load for right now. I think it's best if you drop the group for now, because I care more about you than the group meeting. I don't want to see you get burned out. You're more important."

The leader replied: "Thanks! That's an answer to my prayers."

The message of this "prioritizing people over ministry programs" incident spread like a virus of health, healing balm, and concern church-wide. This Pastor rightly cared more about the person than the ministry. Jesus cares about people; they are His "building program".

4. Apathy and boredom.

#3: What are the main giftings needed for a member of a Dropout Recovery Team?

A) The spiritual gift of mercy
B) The spiritual gift of discernment
C) The gift of wisdom.

#4 Creative ideas and strategies for ministry to Dropouts include:

4.1 Crash -Site analysis

Volvo sends teams to fatal crash sites where Volvos are involved, to learn what the force vectors and other factors were, to see if (and where) the protective steel-cage posts broke, how to reinforce the cars better, and how to reduce future fatalities.

What can those of us in church work learn from our church's dropouts? If we're teachable and open, we can learn from our mistakes as well as our successes.

4.2 **"Drop-Out" trading cards:** Consultant Bob Orr states some local area pastors got together, and brought with them separate cards with typed descriptions of those from their separate churches who had dropped out. One Dropout was described per card: his/her contact information, tendencies, past history, interests, life stage etc.

As they read the cards aloud to each other, one pastor would say: "Heh, I'll give him a try, we have a Vietnam Vets stress-rehab group at our church which sounds like just what he needs", or a Christian 12 Step program for such and such, etc. Over 25% of those "dropouts" were re-activated back into one of the other churches.

Does Jesus wants Dropouts back in His Kingdom, even if they're not going to come back to your church? Shouldn't we as well?

4.3: Exit-interviews: Through phone calls, or mailed surveys, (requesting anonymous responses), a church can learn from its "Dropouts" as well as from its successes (meaning, those of its New Converts that became Regular Members, and then Long Term Members.)
Proverbs 9:8 states: "Rebuke a wise man and he will love you; Reprove a scorner and he will hate you."

#5 Further ministry resources to Dropouts should include study of:

1) Assimilating New Members, by Lyle Schaller
2) The Apathetic and Bored Church Member by John Savage.
3) What Should We Do With Church Drop Outs? by Kirk Hadaway.

Chapter 40

Questions to ask your Dropouts . . . and your Dropout Policies:

Questions for Your Church's Dropouts:

1) What could we have done differently (and better than we did) when you were disengaging from our church.
2) What are those going Inactive or Dropping Out from our church currently wishing they could tell the church as to how to make policies and ministry better?

Questions to Ask Your Dropout Policies:

1) Do we have a written policy for Dropouts and Dropout recovery?
2) Do we need to create an Inactive and Dropout Recovery Task Force?
3) How many people have dropped out of our church in the last 1,2, and 5 years who still live in our local church area?
4) The four main reasons people have dropped out of our church are . . .
5) What can we do to lower our Inactive and Dropout rates?

Chapter 41

Tracking: Introductions

Winning the Back Door War is inseparable from God's command in Proverbs 27:23: **"Be thou diligent to know the state of thy flocks."** The diligent shepherd in Luke 15 could catch (and correct) a 1% loss factor(knowing he had only 99 sheep out of his total flock of 100) by counting, and tracking them.

As someone put it so aptly: "If Jesus thought people were valuable enough to die for, aren't they also valuable enough to be counted and missed, pursued and brought back?"

While some foolishly consider counting "unspiritual", to N-0-T count is the far greater indictment in light of our Lord's concern for His sheep and lambs, as epitomized in Ezekiel 34. Second Samuel 24:1 - 10 is used as a rationalization excuse by some, while totally disregarding numerous times Moses was ordered by the Lord God to count the children of Israel, their tribes, flocks, herds, etc.

#1: Name the two basic components of an efficient tracking system:

A) <u>Every person's primary information is vital</u>. Acquire it by phone, visit, interview at the church, or by writing. It should be required on all New Member class applications so it's systematically gathered at least at that point. Otherwise, you can't track them.

B) <u>**You need to establish "triggering criteria" to signify what specific ministry responses take place.**</u> In other words, when somebody's absent once, twice, three times, what happens at your church? Most churches don't have an operative ministry response to these common events.

#2: Name an Information Age means of multiplying any church's "span of care" :

"Telecare", when done properly, is a very productive "High-tech", potentially very "High-Touch" ministry that can greatly increase the "span of care" any church implements. People must feel cared for, or they will go, and find a place providing that care.

Surveys show that female voices garner less hostility in doing both telecare, and in telesurveys. When calling church members to get information, you're going to get a lot less negative feedback if ladies from the church make the calls.

#4 Why is "tracking" people more important now than ever before? Relate to "fiber-board" analogy.

Tracking is much more important now because our society's social fragmentation rate has "gone ballistic". The sense of disconnectedness the average person suffers is higher than ever before in our national history.

When a pine board is cut out of a solid tree trunk, no glue at all is required. But when thousands of fragmented, broken woodchips are being compressed to create fiberboard, is it going to take more or less glue? More glue of course. How much more glue? An almost infinite amount.

One further question: the smaller the fragments, (as the pieces of wood or people's relationships are broken further and further), will it require more or less glue? . More glue, once again.

#5: What are 10 major signs of fully assimilated, healthy church members(or conversely) 10 warning signs signified by their absence?

Some churches use actual "grading cards" in this arena, to point-grade members, as far as: fully assimilated, partial assimilation, or "in danger" of "backdooring" out of their church.

#1 A healthy RM identifies positively with the church's goals.

#2 Faithful worship attendance at least 3 times monthly.

#3 Involvement in a Sunday school class or other small group.

#4 They're taking steps to become involved and stay involved.

#5 They are growing spiritually, not "plateaued" or in decline.

#6 They should have 7 friends in the church.

#7 They are using their identified spiritual gifts in a role or task. Having a ministry at the church, (no matter how infrequently they participate in it), gives them a degree of ownership. This helps the church be (to them) "my" church.

#8 They tithe and give regularly.

#9 They personally participate in the Great Commission. They pray for the lost, and consider their life and words a witness. They invite friends and acquaintances to church.

#10 They refer to the church as "My church", not "their" church.

#6: Describe an easy 5 column vital-sign: tracking system grid

What if you took some of these ten "healthy member" vital signs, and made an easy tracking system for your church.Remember the diagnostic charts doctors place at the foot of a patient's bed in hospitals? This achieves a similar function.

The congregation's names would go down the left column. Horizontally (as headings) across the top of the page would be:

	Worship Service	Sunday School Care Group	Role & Task	Finances	Friends	Total
Smith, Julie	3	0	1	0	1	5
Strang, Dan	4	3	4	4	4	19

Now it would be easy to use this with a number-scoring system to indicate which areas were strong, average, or weak.

This can be easily set up on a computer spread-sheet, but is also easily utilized in a notebook or ledger (if needful).

Let's say that we use a 4 point grade system such as in High Schools. Four signifies 4 times a month(also an A), a grade of 3 = a "B", a "2" would be a "C", and a "1" or "0" would be a "D."

In the above example, Julie Smith is a regular Sunday morning attender, but has no connection with Sunday School or a care group. Column 3 tells us she very infrequently volunteers, gives financially rarely and has very few friends in church.

With a possible total Assimilation "grade/ score" of 20, Julie Smith totals up only a 5. Hers is a "warning" score and her name would go on a special care list, realizing she'll soon go Inactive, unless something changes to improve her church relationships.

In contrast to her, see the scores of the next church member. Dan Strang "scores" a total of 19 points out of a possible 20. He is a healthy, fully assimilated church member.

You could add in many of these "healthy member vital signs"and get a print out of all those with scores as "healthy" above 14. Another selective print-out could record all those who are marginal, (perhaps scores of 9-14), and then a print-out of those needing intensive assimilation care (Scoring 1 to 8)

There is a more in depth way of looking at this point-scoring concept in Bob Logan's "must-read" book, "Beyond Church Growth".

Chapter 42

Tracking Cards and Basics:

Below are some models of tracking and attendance/information cards used at a few growing, Information Age churches. These cover the range of Rick Warren's Saddleback Valley Community Church in Mission Viejo (a church that's 13 years old, running over 5000, and has planted 24 churches) to Harvest Church which grew to 650 in less than three years.

Notice some common elements, and distinct differences betweenboth Old style and New Tracking cards.

Older style tracking cards:

1) Usually just asked for the basic information: Name, address, phone #, city, state, zip. Age grouping. Pretty much predictable i.e "chocolate,vanilla, strawberry."
2) Very "non information-intensive."

New Information Age Style cards: ask (and obtain) much more specific information.

1) They are "user-friendly", meaning less blanks to fill in, and more boxes to check or numbers (and menu items) to circle.
2) **They obtain more information quicker than "old-style cards"**
3) They always seek information as to lst, 2nd, & 3rd time visit.
4) They are "menu-driven", and offer many information fields to pick from.
5) They are multiple-option, (like modern restaurant menus), and intentionally contain more choices than any one person would ever need, or circle all of.

6) New Tracking Cards are used to track RM's attendance as well as that of visitors.

7) They are more specific and precise in information asked. For Example when asking for tel. #. they ask: 'best time to call"

List of Information Age Tracking Card features include:

1) Today's Date ____and which service attended:8 AM,9:30,11,6PM

2) This is my first visit__ 2nd visit__ 3rd Visit__Other:_____

3) **Family Dimensions Section**: (children, married, single, Children at home; names and ages of children, often even birthdates,indicating a high-care level at the church)

4) **A Lifestyle's-Descriptive section**: to circle or check off
   A) ( ) New resident in area
   B) ( ) Regularly attend church at _____
   C) ( ) Looking for a home church
   D) ( ) ____Would or ____ would not mind a home visit
   E) ( ) Would like a free loaf of home-made bread
   F) ( ) Would like birthday card from pastor;Birth date:____
   G) I am guest of _____

5) **Church-Program Listings**: Usually way beyond the generic Childrens, Youth, Mens, Womens:
   ***Yes. I'd like more information on:
   ( ) How to become a Christian
   ( ) I've given my life to God : Now what?
   ( ) New Believer's class
   ( ) Discovering my ministry and spiritual gifts

6. **Please circle the ministry areas you're interested in:**
   ( ) Singles
   ( ) Children Mins.
   ( ) Women's Ministries
   ( ) Jr. High
   ( ) Young Marrieds
   ( ) Men's Ministries
   ( ) Sr. High
   ( ) Care groups

7. **My Decision Today: (please circle all that apply)**
   A.   I'm committing my life to Christ.
   B.   I want to be baptized
   C.   I'm renewing my commitment to Christ
   D.   Enroll me in the next Membership Class # 101
   E.   I'd like to join a small group
   F.   I'm willing to help wherever needed
   G.   I'd like to talk to a staff minister
   H.   Interested in "Discovering Your Spiritual Gift" seminar

8.   Miscellaneous place for comments, and prayer needs:

   _____
   _____
   _____

Information Age churches use Information Age tracking cards, recognize that the key word in the phrase Information Age is the "I " word, not the other word starting with the letter "A".

They realize that Information equals Power, and that the more information flowing both ways, the stronger the bonding between the visitor and their church will be, especially in the crucial first three visits.

A good exercise would be to jot down on your "idea-bank" page, to have your church's Visitor Care Task Force critique your church's tracking card, pinpointing areas for improvement, upgrading and updating it.

Chapter 43

Implementing Change: Some Tips and Helps

A great "Far Sides" cartoon shows a chin-up bar, and the lintel above the bar has been busted with splintered edges protruding every which way. After noticing this, one looks, and sees the guy lying unconscious on the floor directly underneath the chin-up bar.

The non-verbal application is brilliant: "Don't knock yourself out" getting in shape so fast you do more damage than good.

Change is usually produced by either Inspiration or Desperation. It is all too human in every one of us, to hold onto the former way, until the imagined pain of changing is perceived as less painful than the pain of not changing.

Hopefully, reading this book has increased your inspiration quotient, and given hope to lessen the second option.

The contents of this book may take some churches months to even consider, and years to implement. Of course, all the ideas are not for every church.

We don't want people coming up and saying: "Pastor, your sermon on the need for change today was so great that we've held an emergency vote, and called a U-Haul Truck for you. We already have the search committee out on the road looking for our new pastor."

#1 What three New Testament scripture verses use the Greek word 'metamorphosis' and how does it apply to the subject of change?

The Greek word Metamorphosis means "change", transformation, and transfiguration. It is used in Matthew 17, Romans, 12, and II Corinthians 3:17, only three times in the New Testament.

The Matthew 17 passage is the Transfiguration chapter, where Jesus' face was "metamorphosized" and transfigured: it became bright as lightning.

Romans 12:1, 2 is a passage we all know that states: "Be ye transformed by the renewing of your mind." The word Transformed once again also is the Greek word "Transfigured" (or Metamorphosis). We (and our staff, boards, deacons, elders and leadership and entire churches) are all being commanded by God to have our thinking "transfigured" (metamorphosed).

Finally, II Corinthians 3:17 reads: "We all are being transfigured by the Spirit of the Lord from glory to glory." We all need it. We (and our churches) need to continually be transfigured, and transformed.

#2: John Maxwell defines leadership as:

Maxwell, a master teacher on leadership, defines Leadership by saying: Leadership is Influence." Good leadership is marked by producing good "follower-ship." As Maxwell also says: "He that thinketh he leadeth, and no one followeth, only taketh a walketh".

#3: Six major steps for successful "change implementatation" are:

A) Identify something that's wrong.
B) Propose a plan to change, but call it an Improvement.
C) Propose that change through goals, and strategic, chain-of-logic process.

D) Get key people (the "influencers:) in your corner first. Who are the people that others follow in their decisions.

E) Mention past changes, struggles, and victories. "Vision-cast", the change as an improvement."Vision-cast" or (paint word-pictures as to the beneficial future this improvement will provide for the church. People first rejected the King James Bible and they wouldn't bring it on the May Flower.

#4: Discuss the fact that all growth produces change, but not vice versa

Undeniably, for something to grow, things have to enlarge. Inherent in that process is unavoidable change. An abbreviated formula might be: " No change . . . no growth" .

However while all growth requires and creates change, all change does not produce growth. A disease can eat away at a persons weight, and change can take place, but the change is destroying the person.

Brokering positive change is worth the effort. Change, and being a Change Agent (the title of another great book by Lyle Schaller) is not only a good suggestion, it is the direct will of God. Growth in God's Kingdom is not optional, but a divine mandate.

#5: Proverbs 18:15 states that :

"An Intelligent man or woman is always open to new ideas." (Living Paraphrase)

#6: S.M.A.R.T Goals always include which six elements:

When you set goals for your church, you want to utilize whatever will help you achieve Godly success. Below are six elements (or dimensions) that all good goals must include to achieve what you want your church to envision, target, and achieve.

S.M.A.R.T Goals must have these six elements:
1. S.   They must be Specific
2. M.   They must be Measurable
3. A.   They must be Attainable
4. R.   They must be Revisable
5. T.   They must be Time-defined

A sixth, additional element crucial to smart, healthy goals is this: intentionalize **obtaining Goal Ownership** from the people.

People will always work harder to achieve goals and plans they feel they had a part in creating.

Much could be preached on each of these "smart goal" points. For example take the element of being "revisable". Pastor Paul Yongi Cho set a multi-year goal to have Sunday attendance surpass 100,000 by 1980. On an audio-tape, he's admits he failed! When Pastor Cho got within a year, he realized the attainment of the specific numerical goal was close, but that they weren't quite going to make it. However, he did hit it in 1981.

Prior to hitting the goal, when faced with revising the goal, or failing to hit it, Cho made the right choice. He went to his people, and humbly revised the goal openly, right in front of them, not behind their backs. This doesn't shake peoples faith in their leader; it strengthens their resolve to attain the goal.

We need to be able to say, "We're a bit off, but we're close, closing in. We're going to hit it. We're going to add 12 months to the target date, and with God's help, we'll hit it."

Closing Challenge by the Author:

Hopefully, this book is a new beginning to Winning the BackDoor War...at YOUR church! You have acquired many new understandings and strategies, new perceptions and possibilities in assimilating Pre-Visitors, Visitors, New Converts, New and Regular Members, Inactives & Dropouts.

In Luke 5:36-39, our Lord gives a parable about new and old wine, and new and old wineskins: Jesus said: " No man puts new (fermenting) wine into old wineskins (which have lost their elasticity)... lest the expanding new wine burst the old wineskins, the new wine spill out, and both be lost... But new wine must be put into new wineskins."

Clearly, the New Wine represents God's Spirit. As generations (and paradigms) change, passing the baton to new leadership and new methods (new wineskins) presents a dangerous transition point.

It is **NOT** a question of forsaking, or changing the New Wine. Some mistake their methods and the Message. God's Message is never to be changed: it is the New Wine.

Jesus clearly differentiates New and Old wineskins. Jesus is saying the annointing (the New Wine) is different and separate from the wineskins. **The Message is NOT the method just as the Wineskin is NOT the wine.**

The method (or wineskin) is only a means of carrying God's blessing. God will not pour New Wine into old wineskins.

Jesus continues: "No man wants new wine when he has tasted old wine, for he says 'The old is better (is mellow)," *Lk 5:39.*

This book has planted many new ideas in your mind. God wants both new and old wineskins working together in harmony. We must keep old wine in the old wineskins (methods)...but if we fail to receive new wine into new wineskins as well... we will run dry!

Old wine only comes from New Wine. God will ONLY put new wine....into New wineskins! What new wineskins has God brought your way, by means of this book?

> **My prayer is that you... and your church...**
> **will strive to be both a new... and... an old wineskin...**
> **for God's eternal glory!**

Christian Resource Directory (CRD) & Network

Among the six books I've written, only one required several thousands hours and ten years of work. The Christian Resource Directory weighs in at four pounds. Its 750 pages list 20,000 Christian ministry resource listings, under over 400 topics.

It is the largest Christian Resource Directory in print today.

The basic concept is similar to that of Strong's Concordance, (1889). His goal was to make any Scripture in the Bible easily accessible to anyone trying to locate it.

In the CRD, topical Christian resources are made IN-STANTLY accessible, whether dealing with cults like Jehovah's Witnesses, or Mormons, resources for ministry to atheists or New Age devotees, different ministry areas such as hospital ministry, satanists, life tragedies as incest, "S.I.D.S", cancer, AIDS, etc.

Every believer knows there are countless Christian resources (books, videos, audios, ministries, out there.. somewhere. The CRD is a Strongs Concordance to the vast resources of the Body of Christ. Someday we will make it available on floppy disk & modem for computer users to instantly benefit from & network with.

The goal is the same: to help God's people find the help they need... when they need it, wherever they are... and whatever problem they are facing.

The networking of Christian resources and ministries is drastically needed.

You may order your personal and/church's copy by using the order form at the back of this book.

The Cost is an unbelievably low $20.

Believers don't need resource help until its THEIR best friend in a cult, or dying of cancer or anorexia, or suicidal. However, when they do need and want help, when do they want it? Right! Now!

Information On Gainsbrugh Ministries and Seminars

I travel nationally twice a month presenting seminars to help churches "work smarter, not harder."

In my work as a consultant, and information/resource specialist, I travel extensively both to the latest seminars, and to visit the fastest growing and most innovative churches in the country, such as Willow Creek, Saddle Back Community Church, etc.

Ministry services I offer include, but are not limited to:

1. **Staff-Board Retreats:** and leadership planning sessions.
2. **Local church**, city-wide, regional & district-wide **seminars**.
3. **District-wide Schools of Ministry** and Ministers' Institutes. I have done state wide meetings and seminars in Minnesota, Kentucky and Indiana.
4. **Consulting**: This can be part of weekend meetings, or done weekdays with research work done before being on site. Graphing, analysis, problem identification and corrective strategies staff interviews, seminars, etc. can be customized to any pastor's needs.
5. **Sunday Services**: The seminar host church benefits from:
   A. Having me as the Sunday speaker.
   B. Hosting the seminar at their church, triples the number of their folk attending.
   C. The option of having a Sunday afternoon/evening seminar, at which up to 20—30% of a given host church may attend, as compared to the usual 10% who would attend on Saturdays.

____Yes!   Please send me more information on upcoming seminars, and further literature on your ministry.

What is the maximal way we can provide ongoing help
to churches, pastors, and church leadership teams ?
The best answer we've come up with is what we call our:
Pastor's Care Network (or P.C.N.)

WHAT EXACTLY IS THE PASTORS NETWORK?

The Pastors Care Network is the ongoing way for any church
or pastor to connect in an ongoing way with JGM Ministries
to help your church implement the best Backdoor strategies.

PCN Members Receive::

**THE "100 PACK": You receive a nearly $200 value bundle of
our best Backdoor equipping resources** with unlimited
copy rights (for your church) two audio tapes of the 6 hour
**Backdoor War audio seminar. You also receive a 2nd
seminar "Growing Your Church in the 3rd Millennium"
plus a copy of "The Backdoor War" book , a tracking
pack of 20+ Visitor & absentee tracking forms & ideas,
plus unltd copying Of 2 single tapes: "Paradigm Blindness (& how to Prevent It)" as well as "20 Ways to Close the
Backdoor", a reproducible tape on Backdoor teaching.**

THE "QUAD PACK": 4 booklets (with unltd copying) 3 booklets
are on **"Visitor Care"**: "Help Your Greeters Extend A Warm
& Caring Welcome."(67 pages), "Visitor Parking" & "7
Step Hospitality". The **4th** is "Revolutionary Convert Care"

THE 6 HOUR SEVEN BACKDOOR SEMINAR ON VIDEO

THE $10,000 PCN LENDING LIBRARY: At no cost use the PCN
$10,000 Leadership Lending Library. Leadership training
materials, video/audio & workbook series by John Maxwell,
Wagner, Carl George, Rick Warren, Bill Hybels & many more

JG ON YOUR STAFF (ON A LTD. BASIS) for short consult calls

THE TWICE A YEAR "PCN RESOURCER" NEWSLETTER:

THE MINISTRY MENU PACK": Over six different styles of
"ministry menus", listing the individual ministries any
church has on one sheet of paper (or single literature piece)

THE FOUR LEVELS OF P.C.N. MEMBERSHIP ARE:

Level I:	$ 25 a month (1 year commitment) for churches less than 500 Sun AM
Level II.	$ 50 a month (1 year commitment) for churches 500 & 1000 Sun. AM
Level III	$100 a month (1 year commitment) for churches over 1000 Sun. AM
Level IV	$150 one time one year Smaller church level *Only churches 50 or less
	**This level includes all PCN benefits except the Seminar Video series.

THE LEADERSHIP LENDING LIBRARY

THE PROBLEM: A vast inequity exists in America. About 219,000 churches have <u>less than 100 on Sunday morning</u>. Large churches usually purchase Resources, use, and then shelve them. Smaller churches do without; often not knowing the resource exists to help them: WORK *SMARTER* NOT *HARDER*!

<u>THE OBVIOUS SOLUTION: A MEANS OF SHARING RESOURCES</u>
INTRODUCING: THE LEADERSHIP LENDING LIBRARY. God has called this ministry to gather Resources, (Leadership training videos, audio tape series, seminar workbooks, books, etc.) to help Pastors and Churches; **especially the smaller and smallest ones!**

Jonathan Gainsbrugh, author of the largest Christian Resource Directory (20,000 listings under 400-topics) has seen the <u>power of resources</u> to meet Great Commission needs. He has also repeatedly seen the poor, often non-existent allocation of Christian resources, coast to coast. **Answerable cries for help..unanswered! Meetable needs...going unmet!** He has dared to ask and is trying to answer the question: **"What if Christian churches could nationally pool and share resources on common ministry subjects and problems...no matter what that problem might be"?**

THUS: THE PASTOR'S CARE NETWORK (PCN) AND ITS LEADERSHIP LENDING LIBRARY (LLL) WERE BORN

Imagine: The country's largest Christian library, from leaders as: Maxwell, Hybels, Rick Warren, Dobson, Galloway, Cho, Wagner, Carl George, Gary Smalley, Josh McDowell, Dobbins, Ed Cole, and scores of others at your fingertips. For only $25/Mo., your churches missions can bless and "gift" **two Pastors and churches** (50 members or less) each, with a **$10,000 Resource Library**..... and **FULL PCN BENEFITS!**

NOW ADD THE PCN'S "ADOPT-A-CHURCH PROGRAM"

It is our vision, burden and heartbeat to see other churches come alongside this ministry and help 1,000's of small churches of under 50-members.
<u>TO DO THIS, WE NEED YOUR HELP</u>

1) **PRAY:** We covet your prayers. 2) **PRAISE:** Tell us how resources have helped. 3) **PROVIDE RESOURCES:** Donate money, purchase or send resources for us to share with the Body of Christ. 4) **PARTICIPATE:** If in this area, there is always volunteer co-ministry work you can help us with. Out-of-towners can research for us. 5) **PLEDGE TO THIS MINISTRY:** This Vision and Ministry is totally dependent on believers like you and churches like YOURS to join and make it an ever-growing blessing and reality for others.

HOW DO YOU JOIN THE $10,000 LENDING LIBRARY? ONLY BY JOINING THE PASTOR'S CARE NETWORK!